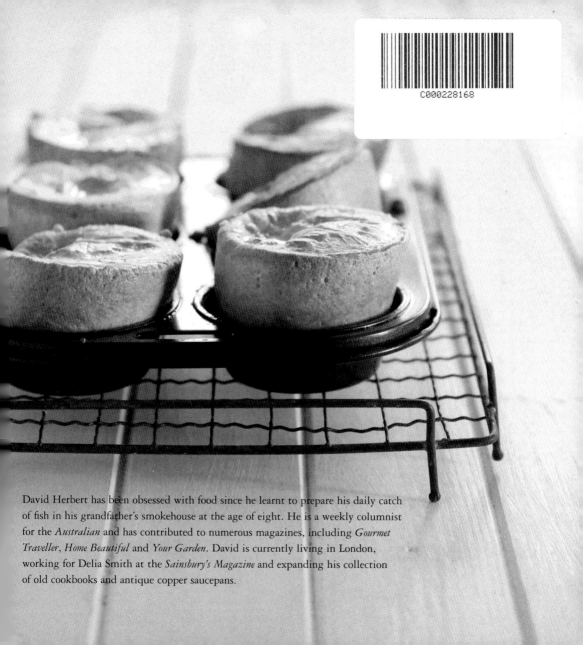

David Herbert has been obsessed with food since he learnt to prepare his daily catch of fish in his grandfather's smokehouse at the age of eight. He is a weekly columnist for the *Australian* and has contributed to numerous magazines, including *Gourmet Traveller*, *Home Beautiful* and *Your Garden*. David is currently living in London, working for Delia Smith at the *Sainsbury's Magazine* and expanding his collection of old cookbooks and antique copper saucepans.

the perfect cookbook

David Herbert

photography by Andre Martin

VIKING
an imprint of
PENGUIN BOOKS

Viking

Published by the Penguin Group
Penguin Books Australia Ltd
250 Camberwell Road, Camberwell, Victoria 3124, Australia
Penguin Books Ltd
80 Strand, London WC2R 0RL, England
Penguin Putnam Inc.
375 Hudson Street, New York, New York 10014, USA
Penguin Books, a division of Pearson Canada
10 Alcorn Avenue, Toronto, Ontario, Canada M4V 3B2
Penguin Books (NZ) Ltd
Cnr Rosedale and Airborne Roads, Albany, Auckland, New Zealand
Penguin Books (South Africa) (Pty) Ltd
24 Sturdee Avenue, Rosebank, Johannesburg 2196, South Africa
Penguin Books India (P) Ltd
11, Community Centre, Panchsheel Park, New Delhi 110 017, India

First published by Penguin Books Australia Ltd 2003

10 9 8 7 6 5 4 3 2 1

Designed by Louise Leffler, Penguin Design Studio
Typeset in Frutiger and Garamond 3 by Post Pre-press Group, Brisbane, Queensland
Printed and bound in Singapore by Imago Productions

National Library of Australia
Cataloguing-in-Publication data:

Herbert, David (David John).
    The perfect cookbook.

    Includes index.
    ISBN 0 670 04051 7.

    1. Cookery. I. Title.

641.5

www.penguin.com.au

For Freya, Rosie, Ella and Rory.
And to Frankie, with love.

an a-z of perfect recipes

introduction

The Perfect Cookbook has grown out of a series of articles originally written for the 'Review' section of the *Weekend Australian*. Each recipe included a method and a few helpful tips. The catch was that I only had 150 words for the whole lot!

Undaunted, I worked away at choosing classic recipes that were interesting and approachable and that would work every time. So began the 'perfect' recipes. The first one I wrote was the 'perfect roast chicken', which is still one of my most requested recipes by readers of the newspaper. I tested the recipe over and over again to make sure it was just right – it took me nearly a week to reduce the method to 144 words. For me, writing the 'perfect' column has been a wonderful exercise in researching, refining, adapting and testing recipes to fit this straightforward format.

This book is a collection of my very favourites from the weekly column over the past couple of years (now expanded very slightly) along with a few new dishes. The recipes reflect my approach to cooking and eating – simple, nostalgic and eclectic, but never fussy or difficult. Anything that was too complicated, too demanding or lengthy did not make its way into the pages. The bottom line was that the recipes had to be foolproof and the dishes had to stand the test of time.

So cook them, taste them, change them to suit your individual taste. Use them as a base to expand your skills. Experiment! After all, it is only food. For the perfect mix, approach these recipes with a sense of fun, not with anxiety. Use good-quality seasonal ingredients and you can't go wrong.

anzac biscuits.

These delicious oat and coconut biscuits were originally made to be sent in food parcels to Australian and New Zealand troops stationed in Europe during World War I. The recipe was created and named for the soldiers of the Australia and New Zealand Army Corps, hence the name Anzac.

1 cup plain (all-purpose) flour
1 cup rolled oats
1 cup desiccated (shredded) coconut
$^3/_4$ cup sugar
salt

$^1/_4$ cup golden syrup
125 g (4 oz) unsalted butter, cubed
1 teaspoon bicarbonate of soda
   (sodium bicarbonate)
2 tablespoons boiling water

Preheat the oven to 180°C (350°F, Gas Mark 4). Line two baking trays with baking paper.

Sift the flour into a mixing bowl and stir in the oats, coconut, sugar and a pinch of salt. Make a well in the centre.

Place the golden syrup and butter in a small saucepan. Stir over low heat until the butter has melted. In a cup, dissolve the bicarbonate of soda in the boiling water and add to the butter mixture. The mixture will foam a little.

Pour the butter mixture into the well in the centre of the dry ingredients and stir with a wooden spoon until combined. Add a little extra water if the mixture is dry.

Drop tablespoonfuls of the mixture onto the prepared trays, leaving 3 cm (1$^1/_4$ in) between each to allow for spreading.

Bake for 12–15 minutes, or until golden. Allow to cool on the trays for a few minutes before transferring to wire racks to cool completely. Store in an airtight container for up to 2 weeks.

Makes 30

apple pie.

1 quantity homemade regular shortcrust pastry (see page 146), or 1 × 380 g (12 oz) packet bought frozen shortcrust pastry, thawed

5 large Granny Smith apples

20 g (³/₄ oz) butter

¹/₂ cup caster (superfine) sugar

1 tablespoon lemon juice

2 tablespoons cornflour (cornstarch)

1 teaspoon ground cinnamon

pinch of ground cloves

1 egg, beaten

caster sugar, extra, to sprinkle

Prepare the pastry according to the instructions on page 146 and refrigerate for at least 30 minutes.

Peel, core and cut the apples into chunks.

Melt the butter in a large saucepan and add the apple, sugar, lemon juice and 1 tablespoon of water. Cook over medium heat for 5–7 minutes, or until the apple has softened. Taste and add extra sugar if needed.

Sprinkle over the cornflour and spices and cook, stirring well, for a further 1 minute. Set aside to cool.

Preheat the oven to 190°C (375°F, Gas Mark 5). Grease a 23 cm (9 in) pie tin or dish.

Roll out two-thirds of the dough between two sheets of baking paper until large enough to line the base and sides of the tin. Line the tin with the pastry, allowing any excess to hang over the sides. Pile the apple mixture into the pastry case.

Roll out the remaining pastry until large enough to cover the pie. Place over the pie and press the edges together to seal. Make two incisions in the centre of the lid for the steam to escape. Trim any overhanging pastry and brush the top of the pie with the beaten egg. Sprinkle the top with the extra caster sugar.

Bake for 40 minutes, or until golden.

Serves 8

apricot jam.

A Sunday afternoon jam session is a great way to preserve your favourite
fruit. Homemade apricot jam is a delicious store-cupboard treat
and is not difficult to make.

1 kg (2 lb) stoned and quartered apricots	1 kg (2 lb) sugar
2 tablespoons lemon juice	

Preheat the oven to 140°C (275°F, Gas Mark 1).

Place the apricots, lemon juice and $1\frac{1}{2}$ cups of water in a large saucepan and bring to the boil over medium heat. Reduce the heat and simmer, stirring occasionally, for 20–25 minutes, or until the fruit is tender and the skin is soft.

Meanwhile, place the sugar in an ovenproof dish and warm in the oven for 10 minutes. Place clean jam jars in the oven to warm also. Put two saucers into the freezer to chill.

Add the warmed sugar to the apricot mixture and stir over low heat until the sugar has dissolved. Increase the heat and simmer gently for 20 minutes, stirring frequently. Skim off any scum that rises to the surface.

Remove from the heat. Drop 1 teaspoon of jam on one of the chilled saucers and return to the freezer for 1 minute. If the jam forms a skin and wrinkles when pushed by your fingertip, it has reached setting point. If not, continue to cook the mixture, testing every 5 minutes, until the jam reaches setting point. Remove from the heat and allow to stand for 15 minutes before bottling.

Spoon the jam into the warmed jars and allow to cool. Seal, label and date the jars. Store in a cool, dark place for up to 12 months.

Makes 6 cups

baked apples.

Cold winter nights are the times to revive this simple, old-fashioned treat.

6 Granny Smith or Jonathan apples

1/4 cup lightly packed brown sugar

50 g (1 3/4 oz) unsalted butter, softened

2 tablespoons chopped hazelnuts

3/4 cup coarsely chopped raisins

1 teaspoon finely grated orange zest

1/2 teaspoon ground cinnamon

2 tablespoons honey or golden syrup

Preheat the oven to 180°C (350°F, Gas Mark 4).

Core the apples, leaving a slightly wider opening at the top than the bottom.

Combine the sugar, butter, hazelnuts, raisins, orange zest and cinnamon in a mixing bowl. Stuff the apples firmly with the mixture and pile any leftover filling on the top. Place the stuffed apples in a baking dish that holds them snugly.

Spoon about 1 teaspoon of honey over each apple. Gently pour 1/3 cup of water into the bottom of the dish and bake for 30–40 minutes, or until the apples are soft.

Serve drizzled with any syrup from the bottom of the dish. Accompany with a jug of thick cream.

Vary the filling by using different dried fruits or nuts. Sultanas and almonds, or dried figs and walnuts, are good combinations.

Serves 6

baked custard.

2 cups milk

1 cup cream

3 eggs

2 egg yolks

1 teaspoon vanilla essence

$1/2$ cup caster (superfine) sugar

$1/4$ teaspoon ground nutmeg

Preheat the oven to 150°C (300°F, Gas Mark 2).

Combine the milk and cream in a medium-sized saucepan and heat gently until the mixture reaches boiling point.

Lightly beat the whole eggs, egg yolks, vanilla and sugar in a bowl. Pour the hot cream mixture into the egg mixture, and whisk well. Transfer to a 6-cup-capacity ovenproof dish and sprinkle with the nutmeg.

Stand the dish in a large baking tin and fill the tin with enough boiling water to come halfway up the sides of the dish. Carefully transfer to the oven and bake for 35–45 minutes, or until the custard has just set – it should still wobble a little. To test, insert a knife about 5 cm (2 in) from the side of the dish; if is comes out clean, the custard is ready.

Serve with fresh or poached fruit.

To make ginger-infused custard, add 1 teaspoon of grated fresh ginger to the cream mixture. Heat and allow the ginger to infuse for 10 minutes. Strain and make the custard as above.

Make individual custards by pouring the mixture into six small ramekins. Bake as above, but for 20–25 minutes only.

Serves 4–6

baked eggs.

This is good as a breakfast dish, or delicious served as a light lunch with a green salad.

½ cup cream
1 tablespoon chopped chives

4 large free-range eggs
salt and freshly ground black pepper

Preheat the oven to 180°C (350°F, Gas Mark 4). Lightly grease four 200 ml (6½ fl oz) ramekins, soufflé dishes or ovenproof cups.

In a small bowl, combine the cream and the chives. Pour equal quantities of the mixture into the four ramekins. Break an egg into each ramekin. Season with salt and freshly ground black pepper.

Place the ramekins in a baking tin and fill the tin with enough boiling water to come one-third up the sides of the ramekins. Carefully transfer to the oven and bake for 8–10 minutes, or until the eggs are set to your liking. These eggs are delicious served with fingers of toasted Turkish bread or brioche.

Baked eggs lend themselves to all sorts of variations. Fresh crabmeat added to the cream mixture is good, as is chopped smoked salmon.

Tarragon, chervil or parsley can be substituted for the chives, if you prefer.

Serves 4

banana bread.

1½ cups plain (all-purpose) flour
1 teaspoon baking powder
1 teaspoon bicarbonate of soda
   (sodium bicarbonate)
¼ teaspoon salt
125 g (4 oz) unsalted butter, softened

1 cup sugar
2 eggs, lightly beaten
2 large very ripe bananas
½ cup buttermilk
icing (confectioners') sugar, to serve

Preheat the oven to 170°C (325°F, Gas Mark 3). Grease a 23 × 12 cm (9 × 5 in) loaf tin and line the base and sides with baking paper.

Sift together the flour, baking powder, bicarbonate of soda and salt.

In a separate bowl, use an electric mixer to beat the butter and sugar for 3–4 minutes, or until pale and fluffy. Gradually add the beaten eggs, mixing well after each addition.

Mash the bananas with a fork and add to the butter mixture. Stir well to combine. Add the combined dry ingredients alternately with the buttermilk, beating well after each addition.

Spoon the mixture into the prepared loaf tin and bake for 55–60 minutes, or until the top of the bread is firm and is a deep brown colour. A skewer inserted into the centre should come out clean. Allow to cool in the tin for 10 minutes before turning out onto a wire rack.

Serve dusted with icing sugar. The flavour improves on keeping. Store for up to 3 days covered in plastic wrap.

Day-old banana bread is delicious cut into slices and toasted.
Substitute a mixture of ¼ cup plain yoghurt and ¼ cup milk if you can't find buttermilk.

beef casserole.

¼ cup plain (all-purpose) flour

1.75 kg (3½ lb) rump or chuck steak,
    cut into 2 cm (¾ in) cubes

⅓ cup olive oil

3 rashers bacon, roughly chopped

8 small brown onions, peeled and quartered

2 cloves garlic, crushed

3 carrots, sliced

2 cups beef stock

2 cups red wine

1 × 400 g (13 oz) can chopped tomatoes

1 teaspoon finely grated orange zest

4 sprigs thyme

1 bay leaf

2 tablespoons chopped flat-leaf parsley

salt and freshly ground black pepper

Preheat the oven to 160°C (315°F, Gas Mark 2–3).

Place the flour in a clean plastic bag. Shake a few pieces of meat in the bag until lightly dusted. Repeat with the remaining pieces of meat.

Heat 2 tablespoons of the oil in a large frying pan over medium heat. Cook the steak in batches, adding a little extra oil if needed, until browned. Transfer to a large casserole dish.

Heat the remaining 2 tablespoons of oil in the frying pan over medium heat. Add the bacon and cook for 2 minutes. Add the onion, garlic and carrot, and cook, stirring occasionally, for 5 minutes, or until the onion is tender. Transfer to the casserole dish.

Drain any fat from the frying pan, add the stock and bring to the boil for 1 minute. Stir to incorporate any bits stuck to the bottom. Transfer to the casserole dish and stir in the wine, tomatoes, orange zest, thyme, bay leaf and parsley. Cover, transfer to the oven and cook for 3 hours. Stir the meat occasionally as it cooks.

Remove from the oven and check the sauce. Add a little extra water if it appears dry. Alternatively, if the sauce is a little watery, uncover and return to the oven to allow the sauce to reduce. Season well with salt and freshly ground black pepper. Serve with mashed potatoes or buttered noodles and plenty of crusty bread.

Serves 6

beer batter.

Batter provides a protective coating that keeps the tender flesh of fish and shellfish succulent and moist. The beer gives the batter a unique flavour and makes it crisp, providing the perfect contrast to the seafood.

1 cup self-raising (self-rising) flour
salt and freshly ground black pepper

1 cup chilled beer

Sift the flour into a bowl and season well with salt and freshly ground black pepper. Gradually whisk in the beer and 2 tablespoons of water to form a smooth batter. Too much liquid added at the beginning makes it difficult to work out the lumps. If lumps occur, pour the batter through a sieve. The batter should be the consistency of cream and can be diluted with a little extra water or chilled beer if needed.

To apply the batter, dry the fish with kitchen paper and completely dip the fish into the batter for a few seconds. Allow any excess batter to run off.

Deep-fry in fresh oil at a temperature of 180°C (350°F) until golden. Do not over-crowd the pan or deep-fryer, or the oil will cool down.

Oysters and peeled and deveined prawns are delicious coated with batter and fried. Try adding a little chilli or curry powder to the flour for a spicier version.

biscotti.

100 g (3½ oz) blanched almonds
250 g (8 oz) plain (all-purpose) flour
1 teaspoon baking powder
250 g (8 oz) caster (superfine) sugar
2 teaspoons finely grated orange zest

1 teaspoon finely chopped rosemary
2 eggs, beaten
1 egg yolk
1 teaspoon vanilla essence

Preheat the oven to 180°C (350°F, Gas Mark 4).

Spread the almonds in a single layer on an oven tray and bake for 7–10 minutes, tossing occasionally, until fragrant and lightly toasted. Cool and roughly chop.

Sift the flour and baking powder into a mixing bowl. Stir in the sugar, orange zest, rosemary and chopped almonds. Add the beaten eggs, egg yolk and vanilla and mix to form a firm dough. If the dough is very sticky, add extra flour.

Knead the dough on a lightly floured surface for 5 minutes, or until smooth. Form into a slightly flattened log about 30 cm (12 in) in length. Place on an oven tray lined with baking paper and bake for 40 minutes, or until firm and golden. Allow to cool on a wire rack.

Reduce the oven temperature to 140°C (275°F, Gas Mark 1). Line two oven trays with baking paper.

With a long serrated knife, carefully cut the log diagonally into 5–10 mm (¼–½ in) thick slices. The slices will be crumbly on the edges, so work slowly.

Arrange the biscotti in a single layer on the prepared oven trays and return them to the oven for 20–25 minutes, turning occasionally, until dry and crisp. Store in an airtight container for 2–3 weeks.

Try substituting pistachios or hazelnuts for the almonds, dry-roasting them as above.

Makes 25–30

boiled eggs.

A boiled egg with toast 'soldiers' is the perfect breakfast. Not only is it compact and nutritious, it's also a great excuse to get the egg cups out of the cupboard. A boiled egg is also a great dish to have for supper if you have had a little too much to eat for Sunday lunch. The cooking time is crucial here – an extra minute on the boil can make a big difference.

4 eggs
salt and freshly ground black pepper

toast, buttered and cut into fingers,
to serve

Place the eggs in a small saucepan and cover with cold water. Bring to the boil over medium heat. Reduce the heat and simmer for 3 minutes for soft, runny eggs, 4 minutes for a firmer set, or 5 minutes for hard-boiled.

Remove the eggs with a slotted spoon and transfer to egg cups. Use a knife to slice off the tops.

Serve with salt and freshly ground black pepper and buttered fingers of freshly toasted bread. Boiled eggs are also delicious served with seasoned salt or zaatar, a Middle-Eastern herb mix, on the side.

To make seasoned salt, combine 2 teaspoons of sea salt, $^1/_2$ teaspoon of freshly ground black pepper, $^1/_4$ teaspoon of ground coriander and a pinch of chilli powder.

To make zaatar, combine 2 teaspoons of sea salt, 1 teaspoon of sesame seeds, $^1/_4$ teaspoon of ground cumin and $^1/_2$ teaspoon of dried thyme.

Serves 2

bolognese sauce.

Serve this versatile sauce with spaghetti, polenta, jacket potatoes,
or simply enjoy it hot on toast.

2 tablespoons olive oil

1 onion, finely chopped

1 carrot, chopped

1 clove garlic, crushed

500 g (1 lb) minced (ground) beef

1/2 cup red wine

2 × 400 g (13 oz) cans crushed tomatoes

1 cup beef stock

2 tablespoons tomato paste

1/2 teaspoon dried oregano

pinch of ground nutmeg

salt and freshly ground black pepper

Heat the olive oil in a large saucepan and gently sauté the onion and carrot for 5 minutes, or until tender and slightly coloured.

Add the garlic and minced beef to the vegetable mixture. Cook until the meat starts to brown. Break up any lumps of meat with a fork.

Add the red wine and cook, stirring frequently, until almost evaporated. Add the remaining ingredients except the salt and pepper. Cook, stirring occasionally, over low heat for 1 1/2 hours.

Season with salt and freshly ground black pepper, and serve.

For a more robust flavour, add 125 g (4 oz) of finely chopped pancetta to the vegetable mixture at the beginning.

Bolognese sauce can be made in large quantities and frozen in small portions for up to 3 months.

Serves 4–6

brandy butter.

Brandy butter, or 'hard sauce', is the traditional sauce that accompanies plum pudding. It can be made up to a week ahead and stored, covered, in the refrigerator. Served cold, it is a delicious contrast to any hot pudding.

250 g (8 oz) unsalted butter, softened
1½ cups icing (confectioners') sugar, sifted

¼ cup brandy
½ teaspoon vanilla essence

Place the butter and icing sugar in a mixing bowl and beat with an electric mixer until the mixture is pale and fluffy. Gradually add the brandy and vanilla, beating thoroughly after each addition.

Transfer to a serving dish and refrigerate for 1–2 hours until firm. Refrigerate until required, or for up to 1 week.

A teaspoon of finely grated orange zest added to the sugar makes a nice addition.

A good but less traditional variation is to replace the brandy with a citrus-flavoured liqueur such as Grand Marnier or Cointreau.

Another way to serve brandy butter is to fill a piping bag fitted with a star-shaped or other decorative nozzle and pipe rosettes onto a plate or tray lined with baking paper. Refrigerate and serve with pudding.

Any leftover brandy butter is delicious on pancakes or spread onto hot raisin toast.

Serves 8–10

bread.

1 × 7 g (¹/₄ oz) sachet (2 teaspoons)
   dry yeast
1 teaspoon sugar

4 cups bread flour
salt
1 tablespoon olive oil

Dissolve the yeast and sugar in a small jug with ¹/₂ cup of tepid water. Stir well and leave for 10 minutes, or until the mixture froths.

Place the flour and a pinch of salt in a large mixing bowl. Make a well in the centre and add the yeast mixture, olive oil and 1 cup of tepid water. Mix until a firm dough forms. Add a little extra water if the dough is too dry.

Knead the dough on a lightly floured surface for 10–15 minutes, or until smooth and elastic. Place in a clean, lightly oiled bowl, cover with a cloth or plastic wrap and leave in a warm place for 1–1¹/₂ hours, or until the dough has doubled in size.

Punch down the dough with your fist to expel the air. Knead on a lightly floured surface for 2 minutes, or until smooth. Place in a large greased loaf tin.

Cover and leave for 45–60 minutes, or until the dough has doubled in size.

Preheat the oven to 200°C (400°F, Gas Mark 6).

Slash the top of the loaf a couple of times with a sharp knife. Bake for 40 minutes, or until the loaf has risen and is golden brown. Turn out the loaf, place on an oven tray and return it to the oven for 5 minutes. When cooked, the loaf should be golden and sound hollow when tapped on the bottom. Allow to cool on a wire rack.

Only use bread-making or strong flour, available from health-food shops or from the health-food section of supermarkets. Alternatively, look for bread flour at growers' markets or a local mill. Plain flour does not contain enough gluten, which gives the dough its elasticity.

Instead of making a loaf, shape the dough into whatever shapes you like and bake directly on an oven tray.

Experiment by replacing some of the white flour with wholemeal or rye flour.

bread and butter pudding.

This perennial favourite dates back to the eighteenth century and is perfect served after a Sunday roast.

30 g (1 oz) unsalted butter, softened

3–4 slices white bread, crusts removed

2 tablespoons orange marmalade

½ cup sultanas or raisins

3 eggs

¼ cup caster (superfine) sugar

1 teaspoon vanilla essence

1 cup milk

1 cup cream

2 teaspoons demerara sugar or raw sugar

Butter the slices of bread. Brush with the marmalade and cut diagonally into quarters. Arrange the bread in two layers in a deep 5-cup-capacity ovenproof dish and sprinkle with the sultanas or raisins.

Whisk together the eggs, caster sugar, vanilla, milk and cream. Pour the mixture over the bread and sprinkle with the demerara sugar. Make sure there is enough liquid to cover the bread – add a little extra milk if necessary. Set aside for 30 minutes to allow the bread to soak up the liquid and to absorb the flavours.

Preheat the oven to 180°C (350°F, Gas Mark 4).

Place the dish in a large baking tin and fill the tin with enough boiling water to come halfway up the sides of the dish. Carefully transfer to the oven and bake for 45–50 minutes, or until the custard is set and the bread is slightly puffed and golden on top.

Add a little ground ginger, freshly grated nutmeg, ground cinnamon or allspice to the cream mixture as a variation.

Substitute chopped dried apricots or figs for the sultanas or raisins.

Use brioche, panettone or light fruit bread for a more sophisticated pudding.

Serves 4

bread sauce.

Bread sauce is a traditional English sauce worthy of a revival. Made of spiced milk thickened with breadcrumbs, it's the perfect accompaniment to roast chicken (see page 132), turkey or game birds.

1 onion, halved
1 bay leaf
3 cloves
4 black peppercorns
1 cup milk

1 cup fresh breadcrumbs
$1/4$ cup cream
pinch of cayenne pepper (optional)
salt and freshly ground black pepper

Place the onion, bay leaf, cloves, peppercorns and milk in a saucepan and bring to the boil over medium heat. Reduce the heat and simmer for 5 minutes. Remove from the heat, cover and allow the flavours to infuse for 20 minutes.

Strain the milk mixture and return the strained milk to the saucepan. Bring to the boil. Stir in the breadcrumbs and simmer, stirring frequently, for 5–7 minutes. Add the cream and cayenne pepper. The sauce should be quite thick. Add a little extra milk or cream if needed to thin the sauce. Taste and adjust the seasoning with salt and freshly ground black pepper.

I often stir in $1/4$ cup of the roasting pan juices as a substitute for the cream.

Makes $1^{1}/_{2}$ cups

caesar salad.

5 rashers bacon, chopped
4 thick slices white bread
1 tablespoon vegetable oil
2 baby cos (Romaine) lettuce
$1/2$ cup freshly shaved parmesan

DRESSING
4 anchovy fillets
1 clove garlic, crushed
2 tablespoons lemon juice
1 egg yolk
$1/2$ teaspoon Dijon mustard
$1/4$ cup olive oil
salt and freshly ground black pepper

Cook the bacon in a large frying pan over medium heat for 5 minutes, or until crisp. Drain on kitchen paper.

Remove the crusts from the bread and cut the bread into 2 cm ($3/4$ in) cubes. Add the oil to the frying pan and fry the bread over medium heat, tossing constantly, until golden brown. Drain the croutons on kitchen paper.

To make the dressing, place all the ingredients except the salt and pepper in a blender and pulse until combined. Season to taste with salt and freshly ground black pepper.

Separate the lettuce leaves, rinse well and dry with a clean tea towel. Place the leaves in a serving bowl, sprinkle over the bacon and croutons, and drizzle over the dressing. Finish with a sprinkle of shaved parmesan.

You can make chicken caesar salad by adding two cooked and roughly chopped chicken breasts to this salad.

Serves 4

carrot cake.

4 eggs, lightly beaten

1½ cups lightly packed brown sugar

¾ cup vegetable oil

⅓ cup golden syrup

1 cup plain (all-purpose) flour

1 cup self-raising (self-rising) flour

1 teaspoon bicarbonate of soda
  (sodium bicarbonate)

½ teaspoon ground cinnamon

2½ cups firmly packed grated carrot

½ cup drained crushed canned pineapple

½ cup chopped pecans or walnuts

Preheat the oven to 160°C (315°F, Gas Mark 2–3). Lightly grease a 23 cm (9 in) round cake tin and line the base with baking paper.

In a large mixing bowl, lightly whisk together the eggs and sugar until the sugar has dissolved and the mixture is frothy. Stir in the oil and golden syrup and mix with a wooden spoon until smooth.

Sift both flours, the bicarbonate of soda and the cinnamon into the egg mixture and mix until smooth. Stir in the carrot, pineapple and pecans or walnuts.

Spoon the mixture into the prepared cake tin and level the top. Bake for 1–1¼ hours, or until golden and firm to the touch. A skewer inserted into the centre should come out clean.

Allow to cool in the tin for 10 minutes before turning out onto a wire rack to cool completely. Serve dusted with icing (confectioners') sugar. Alternatively, spread with cream cheese icing.

To make cream cheese icing, beat 175 g (6 oz) of cream cheese with 60 g (2 oz) of softened unsalted butter until combined. Continue to beat while gradually adding 1½ cups of sifted icing (confectioners') sugar, 1 teaspoon of finely grated lemon zest and 2 tablespoons of lemon juice. Spread evenly over the top of the cool cake.

cheese biscuits.

These crispy cheese-flavoured biscuits are perfect served with a glass of wine or beer. They also make an excellent accompaniment to vegetable soup.

175 g (6 oz) plain (all-purpose) flour
salt
100 g (3½ oz) unsalted butter, chilled and finely diced

125 g (4 oz) cheddar, finely grated
50 g (1¾ oz) parmesan, finely grated

Sift the flour and a pinch of salt into a mixing bowl. Add the butter and rub into the flour with your fingertips until the mixture resembles coarse breadcrumbs. Stir in the cheddar and parmesan. Mix well with your hands until the mixture forms a firm dough, then press into a ball. Alternatively, place in a food processor and pulse until the mixture comes together. You may need to add a little water to make the dough hold together, since cheeses and butters vary in their water content. The dough should be dry but smooth and just hold together without being sticky.

Divide the dough into two portions. With a rolling pin, roll each portion between two sheets of baking paper to a thickness of 5 mm (¼ in). Chill for 10–15 minutes.

Preheat the oven to 190°C (375°F, Gas Mark 5). Line an oven tray with baking paper.

Remove the top sheet of baking paper from each piece of dough and cut the dough into shapes with a cookie cutter. Carefully transfer the shapes to the prepared oven tray. Cook for 15–20 minutes, or until pale gold. Cool on a wire rack, then store in an airtight container.

These biscuits may be made without the parmesan. In this case, increase the amount of cheddar to 175 g (6 oz).

The parmesan may be replaced with gruyère or another firm tasty cheese.

Makes 24–30

cheese soufflés.

100 g (3½ oz) unsalted butter
½ cup plain (all-purpose) flour
300 ml (9½ fl oz) milk
1 cup grated cheddar

2 tablespoons freshly grated parmesan
½ teaspoon Dijon mustard
pinch of cayenne pepper
4 eggs, separated

Preheat the oven to 190°C (375°F, Gas Mark 5). Grease and lightly flour six ½-cup-capacity soufflé dishes.

Melt the butter in a small saucepan over low heat. Add the flour and cook, stirring constantly, for 1 minute. Gradually add the milk and whisk continuously over medium heat until the mixture is smooth, thickens and comes to the boil. Allow to cool for 5 minutes.

Transfer the mixture to a bowl and stir in the cheddar, parmesan, mustard and cayenne pepper. Mix well.

Lightly beat the egg yolks and add these to the cheese mixture. Mix well.

With an electric mixer, whisk the egg whites in a clean bowl until firm peaks form. Fold a quarter of the whites through the cheese mixture to slacken it slightly, then gently fold through the remaining whites.

Spoon the mixture into the prepared dishes and bake for 20–25 minutes, or until risen and golden. Don't be tempted to open the oven until the soufflés have risen. Serve immediately.

The above mixture may also be cooked in a 6-cup capacity soufflé dish. In this case it will take 30–35 minutes to cook.

Gruyère makes a good substitute for cheddar.

Vary the flavour by stirring 2 tablespoons of chopped chives, basil or chervil into the mixture before adding the egg whites.

Serves 6

cheesecake.

250 g (8 oz) plain sweet biscuits
$\frac{1}{4}$ teaspoon ground ginger
125 g (4 oz) unsalted butter, melted
500 g (1 lb) cream cheese
$\frac{3}{4}$ cup caster (superfine) sugar
3 eggs, separated

$\frac{1}{2}$ cup cream
2 teaspoons vanilla essence
1 teaspoon finely grated lemon zest
1 teaspoon lemon juice
icing (confectioners') sugar, to serve

Grease a 23 cm (9 in) springform cake tin and line the base with baking paper.

Place the biscuits and ginger in a food processor and pulse until crushed. Add the butter and process until the mixture comes together. Using your fingertips, press the crumb mixture into the base of the tin and two-thirds of the way up the sides. Refrigerate for 30 minutes.

Preheat the oven to 180°C (350°F, Gas Mark 4).

With an electric mixer, beat the cream cheese and caster sugar until creamy and well combined. Add the egg yolks, cream, vanilla, lemon zest and juice. Beat for 2–3 minutes, or until the mixture is light and fluffy.

Using clean beaters and a clean bowl, beat the egg whites for 3–4 minutes, or until stiff peaks form. Use a large metal spoon to gently fold the egg whites into the cream cheese mixture.

Spoon the mixture onto the prepared cheesecake base and smooth the top. Bake for 35–40 minutes, or until a pale golden colour and just set in the centre. Allow to cool, then refrigerate for 6–12 hours before serving.

To serve, cut into slices and dust with icing sugar.

Serves 8–12

chicken curry.

This is a mildly spiced, easy-to-prepare Thai-style green curry.

1 tablespoon vegetable oil

1 small brown onion, finely chopped

2 cloves garlic, chopped

1 teaspoon grated fresh ginger

2–3 tablespoons Thai green curry paste

1 kg (2 lb) chicken breast or thigh fillets,
cut into 2 cm (³/₄ in) pieces

¹/₃ cup coconut milk

250 g (8 oz) snake beans or green beans,
chopped into 4 cm (1¹/₂ in) lengths

1 tablespoon chopped coriander
(cilantro)

salt

Heat the oil in a large saucepan and add the onion, garlic and ginger. Cook over medium heat, stirring occasionally, for 3 minutes. Add the curry paste and cook, stirring, for 1 minute. Add the chicken and cook, stirring occasionally, for 2 minutes.

Add the coconut milk and bring to the boil. Reduce the heat and simmer gently, stirring occasionally, for 30 minutes, or until the chicken is tender. The sauce should have reduced and thickened by this stage.

Add the beans, stir well, and cook for 10 minutes, or until tender. There should not be a lot of sauce – just enough to coat the pieces of meat. If the mixture is very liquid, increase the heat and simmer until reduced. Use a spoon to remove any oil that rises to the top.

Stir through the coriander and season to taste with salt. Serve with steamed rice.

Vary the amount of curry paste used to suit your taste.

Serves 4

chicken noodle soup.

1 medium-sized chicken

2 carrots, roughly chopped

2 onions, quartered

2 sticks celery, roughly chopped

2 bay leaves

1 tablespoon vegetable oil

1 leek, sliced

1 clove garlic, chopped

2 carrots, extra, sliced

1 onion, extra, sliced

1 stick celery, extra, sliced

100 g (3½ oz) dried fine egg noodles

½ teaspoon grated fresh ginger

salt and freshly ground black pepper

2 tablespoons chopped flat-leaf parsley
    or coriander (cilantro)

2 spring onions (scallions), finely sliced

Place the chicken, carrots, onions, celery and bay leaves in a large saucepan or stockpot. Add 2 litres (64 fl oz) of water, or enough to cover the chicken and vegetables. Bring to the boil, remove any scum and simmer for 1 hour, skimming occasionally.

Remove the chicken and set aside to cool slightly.

Strain the broth, discarding the solids.

Heat the oil in a large saucepan over medium heat. Add the leek, garlic and extra carrots, onion and celery, and cook, stirring occasionally, for 5 minutes, or until tender. Add the strained broth and bring to the boil. Reduce the heat and simmer for 10 minutes.

Meanwhile, strip the chicken meat from the bones and tear into bite-sized pieces. Add to the soup.

Add the noodles and ginger and simmer for 4–5 minutes, or until the noodles are tender. Season to taste with salt and freshly ground black pepper. Ladle into bowls and top with parsley and spring onions.

Serves 4

chicken pie.

1 medium-sized chicken
2 onions, quartered
2 carrots, chopped
1 bay leaf
1 tablespoon olive oil
2 leeks, sliced
50 g (1¾ oz) unsalted butter

2 tablespoons plain (all-purpose) flour
1 tablespoon chopped chives or parsley
salt and freshly ground black pepper
1 egg, beaten
1 × 380 g (12 oz) block frozen
    puff pastry, thawed

Place the chicken, onions, carrots and bay leaf in a large saucepan. Cover with cold water and bring to the boil. Skim off any fat, reduce the heat and simmer for 1 hour.

Remove the chicken from the broth and set aside to cool. Strain the broth, discard the solids and return the strained liquid to the saucepan. Boil rapidly until it has reduced to about 2 cups. Set aside.

Remove the meat from the chicken, cut into bite-sized pieces and place in a bowl.

Heat the oil in a frying pan over medium heat. Add the leek and cook, stirring, for 4–5 minutes, or until tender. Transfer to the bowl containing the chicken meat.

Melt the butter in a small saucepan over medium heat. Stir in the flour and cook for 1 minute. Whisk in the reserved stock. Bring to the boil and continue to whisk until thickened and smooth. Stir in the chives and season well with salt and freshly ground black pepper.

Add enough of the sauce to the leek and chicken mixture to moisten it. Allow to cool.

Preheat the oven to 190°C (375°F, Gas Mark 5).

Spoon the mixture into a large pie dish or tin and insert a pie funnel (if using). Roll out the pastry to a size large enough to cover the pie. Place over the pie, pressing down on the edges to seal. Trim away any excess pastry and use to decorate the top of the pie. Brush the pastry with the beaten egg and bake for 40–45 minutes, or until the pastry is golden and has risen.

Serves 4–6

chicken stock.

Chicken stock is a great base for soups, risottos and sauces, and making your own is simple.

1.5 kg (3 lb) chicken bones (wings, necks
    and giblets are good)
2 unpeeled onions, quartered
2 carrots, chopped
2 sticks celery, roughly chopped

1 teaspoon black peppercorns
3 bay leaves
6–8 parsley stalks
4 sprigs thyme

Place the chicken bones in a large stockpot. Add the remainder of the ingredients and enough cold water to cover by 5 cm (2 in). Bring to the boil, reduce the heat to low and simmer gently for 3–4 hours. Be careful not to let the mixture boil, otherwise the stock will become cloudy. Skim the surface with a spoon to remove any scum.

Strain the stock and discard the solids. Allow the liquid to cool, then refrigerate overnight.

The next day, skim off any fat that has solidified on the top. Refrigerate for 2–3 days, or freeze in 2-cup containers for up to 3 months.

Use the bones left after your next roast chicken, boosted with a few wings or giblets, to make a perfectly good stock.

Try using other vegetables in the stock, such as mushroom trimmings and/or leeks.

Be careful not to add too many carrots, as they can make the stock very sweet.

Leaving the onion skins on gives the stock good colour. But if you want a paler broth, remove the skins.

Makes 2 litres (64 fl oz)

chocolate biscuits.

With chocolate, as with everything else in cooking, the better the quality
of the raw ingredient, the better the end result.

125 g (4 oz) dark chocolate,
   roughly chopped
125 g (4 oz) unsalted butter, chopped

1 egg
1 cup lightly packed brown sugar
1¼ cups self-raising (self-rising) flour, sifted

Preheat the oven to 180°C (350°F, Gas Mark 4). Line two oven trays with baking paper.

Melt the chocolate and butter in a heatproof bowl set over a saucepan of hot water, stirring occasionally, until smooth.

In a separate bowl, beat the egg and sugar with a wooden spoon until combined.

Stir the chocolate mixture into the egg mixture. Add the flour and mix until smooth and thick. Refrigerate for 20 minutes.

Roll teaspoonfuls of the dough into balls and place on the oven trays, allowing 5 cm (2 in) between each for the biscuits to spread while cooking.

Bake for 7–10 minutes, or until the biscuits are firm to the touch and the tops have wrinkled slightly. Cool on a wire rack and store in an airtight container.

As an indulgence, add 1 cup of chocolate chips to the mixture for a dense, rich treat.
To decorate, these biscuits may be spread, dipped or drizzled with melted dark, milk or white chocolate.

Makes 24–30

chocolate brownies.

125 g (4 oz) dark chocolate,
  roughly chopped
125 g (4 oz) unsalted butter, cubed
4 eggs
1½ cups caster (superfine) sugar

1 teaspoon vanilla essence
1 cup plain (all-purpose) flour, sifted
100 g (3½ oz) pecans or walnuts, lightly
  toasted and roughly chopped

Preheat the oven to 160°C (315°F, Gas Mark 2–3). Grease a 20 × 30 cm (8 × 12 in) baking tin and line the base and sides with baking paper.

Melt the chocolate and butter in a heatproof bowl set over a saucepan of hot water, stirring occasionally, until smooth. Allow to cool.

In an electric mixer, beat the eggs, sugar and vanilla for 3–4 minutes, or until pale and fluffy. Beat in the cooled chocolate mixture. Add the flour and beat until smooth. Stir in the nuts.

Spoon the mixture into the prepared baking tin and smooth the surface. Bake for 30 minutes, or until dark brown and the top has formed a crust. Allow to cool in the tin. Remove and cut into squares. Dust with icing (confectioners') sugar to serve.

To make orange and macadamia brownies, omit the pecans or walnuts and stir into the mixture 2 teaspoons of finely grated orange zest and 100 g (3½ oz) of roughly chopped macadamia nuts.

Brownies can be drizzled with melted chocolate or spread with chocolate icing, or frosting (see page 40).

Makes 24

chocolate cake.

This dark, fudgey and delicious chocolate cake is easy to make. It is perfect for afternoon tea or coffee, and packs well for lunch boxes or a picnic.

250 g (8 oz) dark chocolate,
    roughly chopped
250 g (8 oz) unsalted butter, cubed
1 teaspoon instant coffee powder

4 eggs, beaten
$^{1}/_{2}$ cup caster (superfine) sugar
1 cup self-raising (self-rising) flour, sifted
$^{1}/_{2}$ cup ground hazelnuts

Preheat the oven to 160°C (315°F, Gas Mark 2–3). Grease a 20 cm (8 in) springform cake tin and line the base with baking paper.

Melt the chocolate, butter and coffee powder in a heatproof bowl set over a saucepan of hot water, stirring occasionally, until smooth. Allow to cool.

In an electric mixer, beat the eggs and sugar for 4–5 minutes, or until pale and fluffy. Beat in the cooled chocolate mixture until smooth. Gently fold in the flour and hazelnuts.

Pour the mixture into the prepared tin and bake for 50–55 minutes, or until a skewer inserted into the centre comes out clean. Leave to cool in the tin for 10 minutes before turning out. Allow to cool completely on a wire rack before serving lightly dusted with icing (confectioners') sugar.

The chocolate and butter can be melted in a microwave. Cook on medium for 1–2 minutes. Stir until smooth.

Replace the ground hazelnuts with ground almonds, if you prefer.

Make a simple icing (frosting) by melting 125 g (4 oz) of roughly chopped dark chocolate and 40 g (1$^{1}/_{4}$ oz) of cubed unsalted butter. Stir until smooth. Allow to cool. Beat with a wooden spoon until fluffy, then spread over the cooled cake.

chocolate cake (flourless).

250 g (8 oz) dark chocolate,
    roughly chopped
²/₃ cup caster (superfine) sugar
150 g (5 oz) unsalted butter, cubed

1 tablespoon brandy
1 tablespoon strong black coffee
125 g (4 oz) ground almonds or hazelnuts
5 eggs, separated

Preheat the oven to 180°C (350°F, Gas Mark 4). Grease a 23 cm (9 in) springform cake tin and line the base with baking paper.

Melt the chocolate, sugar, butter, brandy and coffee in a heatproof bowl over a saucepan of hot water, stirring occasionally until smooth.

Transfer to a large bowl and stir in the ground nuts. Add the egg yolks, one at a time, beating well after each addition.

In a separate clean bowl, whisk the egg whites until they form medium–firm peaks. Stir a third of the whites into the chocolate mixture to slacken it, then gently fold through the remaining whites with a large metal spoon or spatula.

Pour the mixture into the prepared tin and bake for 45–50 minutes, or until the cake is firm to the touch but still a little soft in the centre.

Allow to cool completely in the tin. The cake will sink a little as it cools. Carefully remove from the tin and serve lightly dusted with icing (confectioners') sugar.

chocolate mousse.

Universally adored and made with just three ingredients, chocolate mousse is equally at home at a dinner party or a simple supper.

3 eggs, separated
200 g (6½ oz) dark chocolate,
    roughly chopped

¾ cup cream

In a small bowl, lightly beat the egg yolks.

Melt the chocolate in a heatproof bowl set over a saucepan of hot water, stirring occasionally, until smooth. Remove from the heat and gradually add the beaten yolks, mixing until smooth. Fold through the cream and stir until combined.

Whisk the egg whites with an electric mixer until soft peaks form. Fold a little of the whites into the mousse to slacken it, then gently fold through the remaining whites. Mix until there are no streaks or pockets of egg white.

Pour the mixture evenly into six small ramekins or cups, cover with plastic wrap and chill for at least 3 hours, or until firm.

Add to the mixture 2 tablespoons of strong espresso and a little brandy or liqueur for greater depth of flavour.

Chocolate mousse can be made ahead of time and kept covered in the fridge for 2–3 days.

Serves 6

chocolate puddings.

This is a simple, quick and easy dessert. As the puddings cook, the batter turns magically into a rich chocolate sauce, topped with a soft chocolate sponge.

1 cup self-raising (self-rising) flour

$^1/_3$ cup cocoa

salt

$^1/_2$ cup caster (superfine) sugar

$^1/_2$ cup milk

1 egg, lightly beaten

60 g (2 oz) unsalted butter, melted

$^1/_2$ teaspoon vanilla essence

$^1/_2$ cup lightly packed brown sugar

Preheat the oven to 180°C (350°F, Gas Mark 4). Grease four 1-cup-capacity ramekins or small pudding bowls.

In a mixing bowl, sift together the flour, half the cocoa and a pinch of salt. Stir in the caster sugar and make a well in the centre.

In a separate bowl, combine the milk, egg, melted butter and vanilla. Pour into the well in the dry mixture and mix until smooth.

Spoon the mixture into the prepared ramekins and place on an oven tray. Combine the brown sugar and the remaining cocoa and sprinkle evenly over the top of each pudding. Bring 1 cup of water to the boil and carefully pour enough of the boiling water over the back of a spoon to fill each pudding to three-quarters. Bake for 20–25 minutes, or until the puddings have risen and are firm to the touch. Serve immediately, lightly dusted with icing (confectioners') sugar.

These puddings are delicious served with thick cream or good-quality vanilla ice-cream.

One large pudding can be made in a 4-cup capacity soufflé dish. In this case, bake for 40–50 minutes.

Serves 4

chocolate sauce.

This easy-to-make, all-time favourite sauce is fantastic served warm
over ice-cream, pancakes, waffles, poached fruit or puddings.

250 g (8 oz) dark chocolate,
   roughly chopped
$^3/_4$ cup cream

40 g (1$^1/_4$ oz) unsalted butter
1 tablespoon golden syrup

Place all the ingredients in a small saucepan over low heat. Stir until the chocolate has
melted and the sauce is smooth.

*Chocolate sauce is delicious flavoured with a little alcohol. Add 1 tablespoon of brandy
or liqueur at the end of the cooking time and remove from the heat.*

Any excess sauce may be stored in the fridge for up to 1 week. Gently reheat before serving.

Makes 2 cups

chocolate truffles.

Chocolate truffles are the ultimate in chocolate treats, and this rich, elegant and highly treasured confectionery is easy to make.

½ cup cream
250 g (8 oz) dark chocolate,
   roughly chopped

40 g (1¼ oz) unsalted butter, cubed
1 tablespoon cognac or brandy
cocoa, to coat

Heat the cream in a small saucepan and gently bring to the boil. Remove from the heat and add the chocolate and butter. Mix with a spoon or whisk until smooth. Add the cognac or brandy and stir well until combined. Cover and refrigerate until firm.

Using a melon-baller or two teaspoons, shape the mixture into balls 2 cm (¾ in) in diameter. Roll each ball between the palms of your hands to smooth them out. If the weather is humid and this is difficult to do, roll them into rough shapes, freeze for 10 minutes and re-roll.

Coat the truffles by tossing in cocoa. The truffles are best eaten fresh, but will keep in an airtight container in the refrigerator for up to 2 weeks.

Be sure to use the best-quality chocolate you can find. It really makes a difference.

Try rolling the truffles in finely chopped hazelnuts, macadamia nuts or almonds instead of cocoa.

Vary the flavour by replacing the cognac with Cointreau, Grand Marnier or cherry-flavoured brandy.

Makes 20

cinnamon toast.

½ cup caster (superfine) sugar

2 teaspoons ground cinnamon

6 slices white bread

50 g (1¾ oz) unsalted butter, softened

In a small bowl, combine the sugar and cinnamon.

Preheat the griller (broiler).

Toast the bread lightly on both sides, then butter each slice, spreading the butter right to the edges. Using a shaker or spoon, sprinkle each slice of toast evenly with plenty of the cinnamon–sugar mixture.

Return the slices to the griller and toast until the sugar starts to melt. Remove, trim away the crusts and cut into quarters. Serve hot.

Any unused cinnamon and sugar mixture can be stored in a screw-top jar.

Serves 3–4

coleslaw.

½ Savoy cabbage or red cabbage,
  finely shredded
2 carrots, coarsely grated
1 red (Spanish) onion, finely sliced
1 clove garlic, finely chopped

3 spring onions (scallions), finely sliced
1 tablespoon olive oil
1 tablespoon lemon juice
salt and freshly ground black pepper
½ cup mayonnaise (see page 98)

Mix together the cabbage, carrot, red onion, garlic, spring onions, oil and lemon juice.
Season to taste with salt and freshly ground black pepper. Stir through the mayonnaise.
Add a little extra mayonnaise if necessary to coat the cabbage evenly.

Coleslaw can be made 2–3 hours ahead of time. Simply cover and chill until needed.

*One to two tablespoons of plain yoghurt or sour cream is delicious stirred into the
mayonnaise before mixing into the coleslaw.*

*To make an Asian-style coleslaw, add 1 seeded and chopped large red chilli, 2 tablespoons
of finely chopped mint and 100 g (3½ oz) of bean sprouts to the salad. Omit the mayonnaise
and make a dressing by thoroughly combining 1 tablespoon of Thai fish sauce, 2 tablespoons
of lime juice, 2 teaspoons of soy sauce, 1 teaspoon of brown sugar and 1 tablespoon of olive oil.
Pour the dressing over the salad and set aside for 10 minutes to allow the flavours to develop
before serving.*

Serves 4–6

corn on the cob.

This is the true taste of summer. Whether you boil or barbecue your corn
on the cob, make sure you eat it with lots of butter, sea salt and freshly
ground black pepper. You are definitely supposed to get messy
when eating corn on the cob!

To boil corn on the cob, discard the husk and silk from the cob and place the cob in a large
saucepan of unsalted boiling water. Add 1 tablespoon of olive oil and boil for 8–10 minutes,
or until a kernel can be pried easily from a cob with the point of a knife. The kernels should
be tender but slightly chewy, with a juicy, sweet flavour.

To grill or roast corn on the cob, strip back the husk, remove the silk, brush the
corn with melted butter or oil and rewrap the corn in the husk. Tie the husk back into
position with string, or tightly twist the husk ends together to secure. Soak in a bowl of
water for 10 minutes. Grill for 15 minutes on a hot barbecue or preheated grill plate, or
roast in a preheated 220°C (425°F, Gas Mark 7) oven for 15–20 minutes, turning every
5 minutes.

*Corn on the cob is delicious served with herb butter (see page 154) or garlic butter
(see page 69).*

couscous.

Couscous is the perfect healthy convenience food and is used in salads,
as well as to accompany tagines or braised dishes. Most varieties available
are precooked and only need moistening and steaming,
so preparation time is minimal.

1 cup couscous	2 tablespoons butter or vegetable oil
1¼ cups chicken stock (see page 36)	salt
or water	

Place the couscous in a medium-sized heatproof bowl and pour over the stock or boiling
water. Add the butter or oil and a pinch of salt. Cover with plastic wrap and stand for
5 minutes, or until the liquid has been absorbed.

If using in a salad or serving at room temperature, simply fluff the grains with a fork. If
serving hot as an accompaniment to a braised dish or tagine, place the bowl containing the
couscous over a saucepan of simmering water for 5–10 minutes, or until warmed through.
Fluff with a fork to help separate the grains.

*Traditionally, couscous is placed in a steamer lined with muslin or cheesecloth and heated
over simmering water for 5–10 minutes to warm through.*

*Chopped mint, coriander (cilantro) or flat-leaf parsley may be folded through couscous
before serving.*

*Make a delicious couscous salad by folding through roasted pumpkin, shredded rocket
(arugula) or basil, finely grated lemon zest, chopped red (Spanish) onion, crushed garlic,
chopped fresh chilli, salt and pepper and a drizzle of olive oil.*

Serves 4

cranberry sauce.

Cranberry sauce is wonderful with turkey or ham, in sandwiches,
or served simply with cheese.

500 g (1 lb) fresh or frozen and thawed
    cranberries
$\frac{1}{2}$ cup orange juice
2 teaspoons finely grated orange zest

$\frac{1}{3}$ cup port
1 cinnamon stick
1–1$\frac{1}{2}$ cups caster (superfine) sugar

Place the cranberries, orange juice and zest, port and cinnamon stick in a medium-sized stainless-steel saucepan and slowly bring to the boil over low heat. Simmer gently, stirring occasionally, for 10–15 minutes, or until the cranberries have burst and the sauce has reduced slightly.

Add the sugar and stir until dissolved. Cranberries can be quite tart; taste and add a little extra sugar if needed. Discard the cinnamon stick. Transfer the mixture to a bowl and allow to cool. The sauce will thicken slightly. Serve cold.

The port may be replaced with water or extra orange juice, if you prefer.
Other spices work well with cranberry sauce. One whole star anise used in place of the cinnamon stick makes an interesting variation.

Makes 2 cups

crème anglaise.

2½ cups milk

1 vanilla bean

6 egg yolks

½ cup caster (superfine) sugar

Pour the milk into a small saucepan. Using a sharp knife, split the vanilla bean in half lengthways. Scrape out the seeds and add the pod and the seeds to the saucepan of milk. Bring the mixture to simmering point over low heat.

In a large mixing bowl, whisk together the egg yolks and sugar for 4–5 minutes, or until the sugar has dissolved and the mixture is thick and pale. Gently whisk the hot milk mixture, including the vanilla bean pod, into the yolk mixture. Return this mixture to the saucepan and cook over low heat, stirring constantly with a wooden spoon, until the mixture thickens slightly to form a custard which coats the back of the spoon. Do not allow the mixture to boil or it will curdle. Remove from the heat and strain into a bowl, discarding the vanilla bean pod.

Serve warm or at room temperature with puddings, fruit pies or poached or fresh fruit. Crème anglaise can be stored in an airtight container in the fridge for up to 5 days. Simply bring to room temperature before use.

A richer version can me made by replacing the milk with half milk and half cream.

Brandy crème anglaise can be made by adding 2 tablespoons of brandy to the mixture after removing from the heat.

Makes 3 cups

cupcakes.

1½ cups self-raising (self-rising) flour
125 g (4 oz) unsalted butter, softened
¾ cup caster (superfine) sugar

1 teaspoon vanilla essence
2 eggs, beaten
½ cup milk

Preheat the oven to 180°C (350°F, Gas Mark 4). Line a 12-hole cupcake tin with paper patty cases.

Sift the flour into a large mixing bowl. Add the remaining ingredients and beat with an electric mixer on low speed for 2 minutes, or until combined. Increase the speed to medium and beat for 3 minutes, or until pale and smooth.

Spoon the mixture evenly into the patty cases. Bake for 15–20 minutes, or until golden and firm to the touch. A skewer inserted into the centre of a cupcake should come out clean. Cool on a wire rack. Ice and decorate as desired.

For orange cupcakes, substitute ½ cup of freshly squeezed orange juice for the milk and add 1 tablespoon of finely grated orange zest to the cake batter. Bake as above.

To make lemon icing (frosting), combine 1 cup of sifted icing (confectioners') sugar, 20 g (¾ oz) of softened unsalted butter and 1–2 tablespoons of lemon juice. Beat until smooth and spread over the cupcakes.

To make strawberry icing (frosting), mash 6 large ripe strawberries with a fork. Combine the strawberries, 1 cup of sifted icing (confectioners') sugar, 1–2 drops of pink food colouring and 1–2 tablespoons of lemon juice. Beat until smooth and spread over the cupcakes.

Makes 12

eggplant dip.

2 large eggplants (aubergines)

3–4 cloves garlic, chopped

2 tablespoons lemon juice

1 tablespoon olive oil

salt and freshly ground black pepper

paprika, to serve

Preheat the oven to 180°C (350°F, Gas Mark 4).

Pierce the eggplants a few times with a skewer. Place in a baking tin and bake for 40 minutes, or until tender. Allow to cool.

Cut the eggplants in half lengthways and scoop out the flesh. Place the flesh in a fine sieve and allow to drain for 20 minutes.

Transfer the eggplant flesh to a food processor or blender. Add the garlic, lemon juice and oil and purée until smooth. Season to taste with salt and freshly ground black pepper. Add a little extra lemon juice or oil if the mixture is very thick.

Serve in a bowl sprinkled with paprika. This dip can be stored in an airtight container in the refrigerator for 2–3 days.

Makes 2 cups

fish cakes.

450 g (14 oz) potatoes, peeled and cut
    into chunks
650 g (1 lb 5 oz) cooked fish fillets, flaked
6 spring onions (scallions), finely chopped
2 tablespoons chopped flat-leaf parsley
    or basil
finely grated zest of 1 lemon
1 tablespoon lemon juice

$\frac{1}{2}$ teaspoon English mustard
1 egg yolk
salt and freshly ground black pepper
1 cup plain (all-purpose) flour
1 egg, beaten
$\frac{1}{2}$ cup milk
1 cup dry breadcrumbs
$\frac{1}{4}$ cup olive oil

Place the potato pieces in a large saucepan of salted water. Bring to the boil and cook for 20–25 minutes, or until tender. Drain and return the potatoes to the saucepan. Cook over low heat for 1–2 minutes to remove any remaining moisture. Mash well.

In a mixing bowl, combine the mashed potato, fish, spring onions, parsley, lemon zest and juice, mustard and egg yolk. Season well with salt and freshly ground black pepper.

Press the mixture firmly into eight patties. Lightly coat each patty in the flour and shake off any excess.

Whisk together the beaten egg and milk in a shallow bowl. Place the breadcrumbs in a second shallow bowl.

Dip each fishcake into the egg mixture and then into the breadcrumbs, making sure each is well coated. Refrigerate for 20 minutes, or until ready to cook.

Heat the oil in a frying pan over medium heat. Cook the fish cakes, in batches if necessary, for 3–4 minutes on each side, or until golden. Serve with lemon wedges, a little homemade mayonnaise (see page 98) and a green salad.

Fish cakes are also delicious made with either tinned or freshly cooked salmon.

Serves 4

fish pie.

1 quantity mashed potato (see page 96)

500 g (1 lb) firm white fish fillets

250 g (8 oz) smoked fish
   (haddock or cod) fillets

2 cups milk

1 bay leaf

4 black peppercorns

50 g (1¾ oz) butter

1 small brown onion, chopped

¼ cup plain (all-purpose) flour

250 g (8 oz) small cooked prawns
   (shrimp), shelled

pinch of cayenne pepper

2 tablespoons chopped flat-leaf parsley

salt and freshly ground black pepper

3 hard-boiled eggs, peeled and quartered

20 g (¾ oz) butter, extra

First, make the mashed potato according to the instructions on page 96.

Preheat the oven to 180°C (350°F, Gas Mark 4).

Place the white fish, smoked fish, milk, bay leaf and peppercorns in a saucepan over medium heat. Bring to the boil then reduce the heat and simmer for 5 minutes. Strain the mixture, reserving the fish and the strained milk.

Skin the fish, remove any bones, flake into bite-sized pieces and place in a bowl.

Melt the butter in a clean saucepan over low–medium heat. Add the onion and cook for 7 minutes, stirring frequently, until soft and translucent. Add the flour, stir well and cook for 1 minute. Slowly whisk in the reserved milk. Bring the mixture to the boil, whisking frequently, until smooth and thick. Allow to cool.

Add the prawns, cayenne pepper and parsley to the bowl containing the fish, and pour over the white sauce. Season well with salt and freshly ground black pepper.

Spoon the mixture into a large soufflé dish or other ovenproof dish. Top with the boiled egg pieces. Spread with the mashed potato and fluff up with a fork. Dot with the extra butter. Bake for 30–35 minutes, or until golden and bubbling.

Serves 4–6

french toast.

These slices of thick bread, dipped in a rich mix of egg, milk, sugar and vanilla, make a delicious, indulgent start to the day – especially when delivered to your bed on a tray.

4 eggs

2 tablespoons caster (superfine) sugar

$^1/_2$ cup milk or cream

$^1/_2$ teaspoon vanilla essence

salt

1 white cob or cottage loaf

unsalted butter, for frying

maple syrup, to serve

In a shallow bowl, mix together the eggs, sugar, milk, vanilla and a pinch of salt.

Cut four slices of bread, about 2 cm ($^3/_4$ in) thick, from the loaf of bread.

Heat a little butter in a frying pan over medium heat. Dip two slices of bread in the egg mixture for 30–60 seconds, or until the mixture is well absorbed by the bread. Fry the soaked bread for 1 minute on each side, or until crisp and golden. Repeat with the remaining slices of bread.

Serve warm, drizzled with maple syrup.

French toast is delicious served with a little crispy bacon or fresh berries on the side. Slices of brioche or split croissants instead of the bread make a good variation.

Serves 2

friands.

These delicious, moist almond cakes are easy to make at home.

180 g (6 oz) unsalted butter

⅓ cup plain (all-purpose) flour

180 g (6 oz) icing (confectioners') sugar

100 g (3½ oz) ground almonds

2 teaspoons finely grated lemon zest

5 egg whites

icing (confectioners') sugar, extra,
   to serve

Preheat the oven to 200°C (400°F, Gas Mark 6). Lightly grease eight friand tins.

Melt the butter in a small saucepan over low heat, then cook for a further 1 minute, or until golden. Be careful not to burn the butter.

Sift the flour and icing sugar into a mixing bowl. Stir in the ground almonds and lemon zest.

Lightly beat the egg whites with a fork and pour into the bowl containing the dry ingredients. Add the warm butter and mix with a wooden spoon until smooth.

Spoon the mixture into the prepared friand tins, filling each to three-quarters full. Bake for 5 minutes, then reduce the heat to 180°C (350°F, Gas Mark 4) and cook for a further 10–15 minutes, or until golden and risen.

Allow to cool in the tins for 5 minutes before turning out onto a wire rack to cool completely. Dust with icing sugar to serve.

If you don't have friand tins, bake these little cakes in muffin tins or deep patty pan tins. In place of the lemon zest, try orange zest.

To make berry friands, top each with a few fresh or frozen raspberries, blackberries or blueberries before baking.

Makes 8

fried rice.

The recipe for this favourite Cantonese dish can be readily varied,
depending on what ingredients are at hand.

1 tablespoon vegetable oil

2 eggs, lightly beaten

2 tablespoons peanut oil

5 spring onions (scallions), chopped

1 clove garlic, crushed

$\frac{1}{2}$ cup frozen peas, thawed

1 tablespoon grated fresh ginger

1 cup shredded Chinese barbecue pork

4 cups cooked rice, chilled

1 tablespoon of soy sauce or XO sauce

salt and ground white pepper

Heat the vegetable oil in a moderately hot wok and add the beaten egg, swirling it around
to coat the wok. When set, turn out onto a board and allow to cool. Cut into strips.

Heat the peanut oil in the wok. Add the spring onions, garlic, peas and ginger. Stir-fry
for 2–3 minutes. Add the pork and allow to warm through. Add the rice and egg strips. Stir-
fry vigorously, breaking up any lumps or rice, until heated through. Add the soy sauce and
mix until well combined. Season with salt and ground white pepper and serve immediately.

*Always begin with cold rice cooked the day before. Boil 2 cups of long-grain rice in
a large saucepan of boiling salted water for 10–15 minutes, or until tender. When cooked,
drain and rinse. Store overnight in the refrigerator.*

*Chinese barbecue pork is available in Asian food stores and restaurants. If it is
unavailable, substitute chopped ham, chopped cooked bacon or chopped cooked chicken.*

*Peeled, cooked prawns (shrimp) added towards the end of the cooking time are also
delicious in this dish.*

Serves 4

frittata.

Frittatas can vary from thin and pancake-like to thick with a golden crust and creamy centre. The following recipe for this popular Italian omelette is a classic flavour combination and is perfect picnic fare.

6 large eggs

100 g (3½ oz) baby spinach leaves,
   roughly chopped

1¼ cups freshly grated parmesan

pinch of freshly grated nutmeg

salt and freshly ground black pepper

1 tablespoon olive oil

In a mixing bowl, beat the eggs lightly with a fork. Stir through the spinach, 1 cup of the parmesan and the nutmeg. Season to taste with salt and freshly ground black pepper.

Heat the olive oil in a 23 cm (9 in) non-stick frying pan over medium heat. Swirl the pan to coat with oil. Pour in the egg mixture. Reduce the heat to low and cook, stirring once, for 12–15 minutes. The bottom should be firm and the top a little runny. Sprinkle with the remaining ¼ cup of parmesan.

Place the frying pan under a preheated griller (broiler) for just long enough to set the top. A good frittata should be firm but moist, never stiff and dry. Remove from the heat and allow to cool for 2 minutes. Serve straight from the pan, or place a large, flat plate over the top of the pan and invert the frittata onto it. Serve warm or at room temperature, sliced into wedges.

Variations on this recipe are only limited by what ingredients you have at hand. Try incorporating cooked zucchini (courgettes), sautéed mushrooms, cooked asparagus, prosciutto, marinated artichokes, goat's cheese or cooked potato slices.

Serves 4

fruit cake.

250 g (8 oz) unsalted butter, chopped

1 cup lightly packed brown sugar

1/2 cup brandy

1 kg (2 lb) mixed dried fruit

100 g (3 1/2 oz) mixed peel

100 g (3 1/2 oz) glacé cherries, halved

5 eggs, beaten

2 tablespoons treacle

2 teaspoons finely grated lemon zest

2 tablespoons finely grated orange zest

1 3/4 cups plain (all-purpose) flour

1/2 cup self-raising (self-rising) flour

1 teaspoon bicarbonate of soda
    (sodium bicarbonate)

1 1/2 teaspoons mixed spice

150 g (5 oz) almonds

Place the butter, sugar, brandy, dried fruit, mixed peel, glacé cherries and 1/2 cup of water in a large saucepan. Bring to the boil and simmer gently, stirring frequently, for 10 minutes. Allow to cool.

Preheat the oven to 150°C (300°F, Gas Mark 2). Grease a 23 cm (9 in) round cake tin. Line the base and sides with a double layer of baking paper, extending the paper 5 cm (2 in) above the cake tin.

Transfer the cool fruit mixture to a large mixing bowl. Add the beaten eggs, treacle, lemon and orange zest, and mix well. Sift the flours, bicarbonate of soda and mixed spice into the bowl and mix until combined. Roughly chop half the almonds and stir these into the mixture. Spoon the mixture into the prepared cake tin. Decorate the top of the cake with the remaining whole almonds. Wrap the cake tin in a double layer of brown paper, extending the paper 5 cm (2 in) above the cake tin, to match the baking paper. Tie securely with string.

Bake for 2–2 1/2 hours, or until firm and a skewer inserted into the centre comes out clean. Allow to cool in the tin. Wrap in foil and store for up to 3 months in a cool, dark place.

A good combination of mixed dried fruit is 375 g (12 oz) of chopped raisins, 250 g (8 oz) of sultanas, 250 g (8 oz) of currants, and 125 g (4 oz) of chopped dates, figs and prunes.

fruit tart.

2 tablespoons apricot jam

1 sheet frozen puff pastry, thawed

3 ripe nectarines or plums

2 tablespoons sugar

20 g (³/₄ oz) unsalted butter

Preheat the oven to 200°C (400°F, Gas Mark 6).

Place the jam and 2 tablespoons of water in a small saucepan and warm until the mixture forms a syrup. Brush half the syrup over the sheet of pastry, leaving a 2 cm (³/₄ in) border all around.

Halve the nectarines or plums, remove the seeds and thinly slice the fruit. Lay the slices, overlapping slightly, over the pastry, again leaving a 2 cm (³/₄ in) border all around. Sprinkle over the sugar and dot the fruit with the butter.

Bake the tart for 20–25 minutes, or until the pastry is golden and puffed up. Glaze the tart by brushing lightly with the remaining jam. Cut into slices and serve warm or at room temperature with cream or ice-cream.

Two peeled and thinly sliced pears or apples may be substituted for the stone fruit.

Serves 4

garlic bread.

1 baguette or bread stick
salt and freshly ground black pepper

GARLIC BUTTER
200 g (6½ oz) unsalted butter, softened
4 cloves garlic, chopped
2 tablespoons finely chopped
    flat-leaf parsley
1 teaspoon lemon juice

Preheat the oven to 180°C (350°F, Gas Mark 4).

To make the garlic butter, mix together the ingredients thoroughly in a small mixing bowl. Season with salt and freshly ground black pepper.

Cut slashes into the baguette at 2.5 cm (1 in) intervals, cutting almost to the bottom crust, and spread each side of the cut liberally with the garlic butter.

Wrap the bread in foil and bake for 10 minutes. Open the foil at the top and cook for another 5–7 minutes, or until crisp. Serve immediately.

Any leftover garlic butter can be rolled in foil and kept in the fridge for up to 2 weeks.
Add a little finely chopped chilli or a dash of Tabasco sauce to the garlic butter for
a hotter version.

Serves 4

garlic prawns.

The combination of butter, garlic and parsley is a true classic.

24 large uncooked prawns (shrimp)
80 g (2¾ oz) unsalted butter
2 tablespoons olive oil
3 cloves garlic, finely chopped
½ large red chilli, seeded and
    finely chopped

2 tablespoons chopped flat-leaf parsley
juice of 1 lemon
sea salt and freshly ground black pepper
1 tablespoon chopped flat-leaf
    parsley, extra
2 teaspoons finely grated lemon zest

Peel and devein the prawns, leaving the tails intact. Set aside.

Melt the butter and olive oil in a large frying pan or wok over medium heat. Add the garlic and chilli and cook, stirring, for 3 minutes. Add the prawns and cook, untouched, for 2 minutes. Turn the prawns, add the parsley and squeeze over the lemon juice. Cook for a further 2–3 minutes, or until the prawns are pink. Season with sea salt and freshly ground black pepper.

In a small bowl, combine the extra chopped parsley and the lemon zest, and sprinkle this mixture over the prawns. Serve at once with good crusty bread to mop up the juices.

As a variation, add ½ teaspoon of grated fresh ginger at the beginning with the garlic and chilli. Cook as above, but replace the lemon with lime, and the parsley with coriander (cilantro). Fresh scallops are also delicious cooked this way.

Serves 4

gazpacho.

Few dishes taste as refreshing on a hot summer's day as this simple, no-cook, chilled soup.

1 kg (2 lb) ripe tomatoes, peeled and
    chopped
1 small cucumber, roughly chopped
1 red capsicum (bell pepper), seeded
    and chopped
2 cloves garlic, chopped

$^{1}/_{2}$ red (Spanish) onion, chopped
2 thick slices good white bread
$^{1}/_{4}$ cup sherry vinegar or red wine vinegar
salt and freshly ground black pepper
extra-virgin olive oil, to drizzle

Place the tomatoes, cucumber, capsicum, garlic and onion in a large mixing bowl. Remove the crusts from the bread. Chop the bread and add it to the bowl. Stir through $1^{1}/_{2}$ cups of water.

Transfer the mixture to a food processor or blender and pulse until the mixture is roughly combined. (This may need to be done in batches.) The mixture should still be slightly chunky. Add a little extra water if the soup needs thinning.

Chill for at least 2 hours, or preferably overnight, to allow the flavours to develop.

Just before serving, stir through the vinegar. Season to taste with salt and freshly ground black pepper. Serve well chilled with a good drizzle of extra-virgin olive oil.

To peel tomatoes, use a sharp knife to cut a cross in the base of each tomato. Place in a heatproof bowl and cover with boiling water. Leave for 45 seconds, then transfer to cold water and peel the skin away, beginning at the cross.

Decent tomatoes are essential for a good gazpacho. If possible, use home-grown ones.

Crabmeat or cooked prawns are delicious additions to this soup.

Serves 4

ginger cake.

This cake is a great addition to your recipe collection. It's delicious and easy to make – it falls into that stress-free 'melt and mix' category of baking.

60 g (2 oz) unsalted butter, cubed

$^{1}/_{2}$ cup golden syrup

$^{3}/_{4}$ cup plain (all-purpose) flour

$^{1}/_{4}$ cup self-raising (self-rising) flour

1 teaspoon bicarbonate of soda (sodium bicarbonate)

1 heaped teaspoon ground ginger

$^{1}/_{2}$ teaspoon mixed spice

$^{1}/_{2}$ cup caster (superfine) sugar

salt

$^{1}/_{2}$ cup milk

1 egg, beaten

Preheat the oven to 170°C (325°F, Gas Mark 3). Thoroughly grease a 23 × 12 cm (9 × 5 in) loaf tin and line the base with baking paper.

Place the butter and golden syrup in a small saucepan. Melt, stirring occasionally, over low heat. Remove from the heat.

Sift both flours, the bicarbonate of soda and the spices into a mixing bowl. Stir in the sugar and a pinch of salt, then add the milk and egg and mix until smooth. Gradually add the melted butter mixture, stirring until well incorporated.

Pour the batter into the prepared loaf tin and bake for 50–55 minutes, or until risen and firm to the touch. A skewer inserted into the middle of the cake should come out clean. Allow the cake to cool in the tin for 5 minutes before turning out onto a wire rack to cool. Serve dusted with icing (confectioners') sugar.

If you like, you can turn this into a simple syrup cake. Place $^{1}/_{2}$ cup of sugar, $^{1}/_{2}$ cup of water and 1 tablespoon of finely grated fresh ginger in a small saucepan. Bring the mixture to the boil and simmer for 5 minutes. Spoon a little syrup over the hot cake.

gingerbread biscuits.

125 g (4 oz) unsalted butter

¼ cup golden syrup

⅓ cup lightly packed brown sugar

2 cups plain (all-purpose) flour

¼ cup self-raising (self-rising) flour

1 tablespoon bicarbonate of soda (sodium bicarbonate)

1 tablespoon ground ginger

½ teaspoon mixed spice

salt

1 egg, lightly beaten

Place the butter, golden syrup and sugar in a small saucepan over low heat. Cook, stirring, until the butter has melted and the mixture is smooth. Remove from the heat and allow to cool.

Sift both flours, the bicarbonate of soda, the spices and a pinch of salt into a large mixing bowl and make a well in the centre. Pour in the melted butter mixture and the beaten egg and mix well.

Turn out onto a lightly floured surface and knead until smooth. Wrap in plastic wrap and refrigerate for 30 minutes.

Preheat the oven to 170°C (325°F, Gas Mark 3). Line two oven trays with baking paper.

Roll out the dough between two sheets of baking paper to a thickness of 5 mm (¼ in). Cut out shapes with cookie cutters and bake for 8–10 minutes, or until firm and golden brown. Allow to cool on a wire rack.

To decorate your biscuits, beat 1 egg white with an electric mixer until foamy. Gradually add 1 teaspoon of lemon juice and 1½ cups of sifted icing (confectioners') sugar, beating all the while until the mixture is thick and smooth. Tint the mixture with a couple of drops of food colouring. Attach a fine nozzle to a piping bag and pipe decorative shapes onto the biscuits.

Makes 24–30

granola.

The perfect granola should be chewy, crisp and crumbly, with a combination of sweet and tart flavours. The trick is selecting the right ingredients and combining them in the proper proportions. Try this basic recipe, substituting different nuts, seeds or fruit as desired.

3 cups rolled oats

1 cup almonds

$1/2$ cup roughly chopped pecans

$1/2$ cup shredded coconut

2 tablespoons sesame seeds

2 tablespoons pepitas (pumpkin seeds)

$1/4$ cup wheatgerm

1 teaspoon finely grated lemon zest

$1/3$ cup vegetable oil

$1/2$ cup honey

1 cup chopped dried apricots

1 cup sultanas

Preheat the oven to 170°C (325°F, Gas Mark 3).

Place the oats, almonds, pecans, coconut, sesame seeds, pepitas, wheatgerm and lemon zest in a large mixing bowl.

In a small saucepan over low heat, warm the vegetable oil and honey.

Pour the honey mixture over the oat mixture and mix thoroughly.

Tip the mixture into a baking tin and bake, stirring every 5 minutes, for 20 minutes, or until golden. Allow the mixture to cool completely.

Stir through the apricots and sultanas.

Granola can be stored in an airtight container for up to 3 months.

When experimenting with different combinations of ingredients, keep in mind that the total volume of nuts and fruit should be equal to or slightly greater than the volume of oats.

Vary the dried fruit component by using dried apples, pears or peaches.

Makes 8 cups

gravy.

pan juices from roast meat
2–3 tablespoons plain (all-purpose) flour
$^1/_2$ cup wine

2 cups stock or water
salt and freshly ground black pepper

After removing the roast meat from the baking tin, pour off all but about $^1/_2$ cup of the fat. Place the baking tin over medium heat on the stove top and sprinkle over the flour. Stir constantly with a wooden spoon for 1–2 minutes, or until the flour has browned slightly.

Gradually add the wine and stock, stirring constantly to loosen any browned bits stuck to the bottom of the tin, until the gravy has thickened and is smooth. Simmer gently for 5–10 minutes, adding a little extra stock or water if necessary to reach the desired consistency. Season to taste with salt and freshly ground black pepper.

As a rule, use white wine to make gravy for poultry dishes and red wine for red meat dishes.

Serves 4–6

guacamole.

2 ripe avocados
juice of 2 limes
1 large green chilli, seeded
    and finely chopped

¼ cup finely chopped flat-leaf parsley
    or coriander (cilantro)
3 spring onions (scallions), finely chopped
1 tablespoon olive oil
salt and freshly ground black pepper

Peel and seed the avocados, and roughly chop the flesh. Transfer to a small bowl. Add the lime juice, chilli, parsley or coriander and spring onions. Mash together with a fork, gradually incorporating the olive oil.

Season to taste with salt and freshly ground black pepper, and add a little extra lime juice if needed.

Add 2–3 drops of Tabasco sauce if you like a hotter guacamole.

Makes 1 cup

hollandaise sauce.

Hollandaise sauce is wonderful served with fish, steamed asparagus or with poached eggs, as in eggs Benedict.

125 g (4 oz) unsalted butter
1 tablespoon lemon juice

3 egg yolks
salt and freshly ground black pepper

Melt the butter in a small saucepan over low heat. Pour the melted butter into a small jug, leaving behind any white sediment in the bottom of the pan. Allow to cool slightly.

Place the lemon juice, egg yolks and 1 tablespoon of water in a heatproof bowl over a saucepan of simmering water. Whisk the yolk mixture until combined. Gradually add the melted butter, whisking until the sauce is smooth and thick. If the sauce thickens too much, whisk in a spoonful of hot water. Do not allow the mixture to boil or the sauce will separate. Season to taste with salt and freshly ground black pepper, and keep warm until ready to serve.

You can make hollandaise sauce in a food processor or blender by processing the lemon juice, egg yolks and 1 tablespoon of water in the machine. While the machine is running, gradually add the warm melted butter until the sauce is smooth and thick. Season to taste with salt and freshly ground black pepper.

To make orange hollandaise, replace the lemon juice with 2 tablespoons of strained freshly squeezed orange juice and proceed as above.

Makes 1 cup

hot chocolate.

The perfect hot chocolate isn't made from powder spooned from a tin,
it's made using real chocolate. Hot chocolate should be very rich –
wonderful for a cold, wintry night.

2 cups milk

100 g (3½ oz) dark chocolate, chopped

sugar, to taste

Gently heat the milk in a saucepan over low heat for 2 minutes. Add the chocolate and stir occasionally, until melted and smooth. Bring the mixture to just under boiling point and whisk briskly for a couple of minutes to make it frothy.

Taste for sweetness and stir in a little sugar if needed. Pour the hot chocolate into cups and serve immediately.

For an extra treat, add marshmallows to the cup before pouring over the hot chocolate. Or try topping with a dollop of lightly whipped cream and sprinkling with a little coarsely grated chocolate.

For extra richness, use couverture chocolate, which has a high cocoa butter content and melts beautifully.

Serves 2

hummus.

1 × 425 g (14 oz) can chickpeas (garbanzo
beans), drained and rinsed

3 cloves garlic, crushed

¼ cup lemon juice

¼ cup tahini (sesame paste)

1 teaspoon ground cumin

pinch cayenne pepper

¼ cup olive oil

salt and freshly ground black pepper

Place the chickpeas, garlic, lemon juice, tahini, cumin and cayenne pepper in the bowl of a food processor. With the motor running, slowly add the olive oil and process until smooth. Add a little extra oil or lemon juice if the mixture is too thick. Season to taste with salt and freshly ground black pepper.

Serve with pita bread. Leftover hummus can be stored in an airtight container in the refrigerator for 2–3 days.

Makes 1 cup

jelly.

This recipe is a grown-up version of that favourite wobbly, nostalgic treat.
Fresh fruit jelly is delicious served with good-quality ice-cream.

1 litre (32 fl oz) freshly squeezed orange
    juice, strained
2 × 10 g (¼ oz) sachets (1½ tablespoons)
    powdered gelatine

2–3 tablespoons sugar
¼ cup Grand Marnier

Place 1 cup of the orange juice in a small bowl, sprinkle over the gelatine and leave
to soften for 5 minutes.

Bring the remaining juice to the boil in a medium-sized saucepan. Taste and add sugar
until the jelly is sweet enough for you. Stir until the sugar has dissolved. Remove from the
heat and stir through the softened gelatine mixture until it has completely dissolved. Add
the Grand Marnier and mix well.

Pour the mixture into small individual decorative moulds, or simply into a bowl or
shallow dish. Allow to cool to room temperature. Refrigerate for 3–4 hours until set, and
turn out. Serve with ice-cream.

*Any fresh fruit juice or juice combination can be used in this recipe – all except pineapple
juice, which inhibits the gelatine setting.*

*Delicious jellies can be made using store-bought cranberry or berry juices and substituting
schnapps or vodka for the Grand Marnier.*

Fresh raspberries or strawberries can be set in the jelly.

*Use powdered or leaf gelatine, depending on what is available. Six leaves will set 1 litre
(32 fl oz) of liquid.*

Serves 6

lamingtons.

CAKE

150 g (5 oz) unsalted butter, softened

1¾ cups self-raising (self-rising) flour

1 teaspoon baking powder

1 cup caster (superfine) sugar

3 eggs, lightly beaten

1 teaspoon vanilla essence

½ cup milk

COATING

3 cups icing (confectioners') sugar

⅓ cup cocoa

30 g (1 oz) unsalted butter, melted

¾ cup milk

3 cups desiccated (shredded) coconut

Preheat the oven to 180°C (350°F, Gas Mark 4). Grease a 20 × 30 cm (8 × 12 in) shallow cake tin and line the base with baking paper.

Place all the cake ingredients in a large mixing bowl and beat with an electric mixer on medium speed for 3 minutes, or until the mixture is smooth. Spoon into the prepared tin and smooth the surface.

Bake for 45–50 minutes, or until golden and firm to the touch. Allow to cool in the tin for 5 minutes before turning out onto a wire rack to cool completely.

Make the coating by sifting the icing sugar and cocoa into a heatproof bowl. Stir in the melted butter and milk. Place the bowl over a saucepan of simmering water and stir until smooth and shiny. Remove from the heat. The mixture should be thin – add a little boiling water if necessary.

Place the coconut in a shallow bowl.

Trim away the edges of the cool cake and cut the cake lengthways into three even strips. Cut each strip into eight even pieces. Using two forks, dip each piece of cake into the chocolate mixture then roll in the coconut. Transfer to a wire rack to dry. Repeat with the remaining pieces of cake.

Makes 24

lasagne.

50 g (1¾ oz) unsalted butter

⅓ cup plain (all-purpose) flour

2½ cups milk

pinch of freshly grated nutmeg

salt and freshly ground black pepper

500 g (1 lb) fresh lasagne sheets (noodles)

1 quantity bolognese sauce (see page 18)

¾ cup freshly grated parmesan

Melt the butter in a medium-sized saucepan and stir in the flour. Cook over medium heat, stirring constantly, for 1 minute. Remove from the heat and gradually add the milk, stirring constantly. Return to the heat and bring to the boil, stirring frequently. Simmer for 2 minutes, or until the sauce has thickened. Add the nutmeg and season well with salt and freshly ground black pepper. Set aside.

Cook the lasagne sheets, two at a time, in a large saucepan of boiling salted water for 2 minutes. Remove and refresh by placing in a large bowl of iced water for 2 minutes. Dry well with kitchen paper.

Preheat the oven to 180°C (350°F, Gas Mark 4). Lightly grease a 30 × 21 × 5 cm (12 × 8½ × 2 in) ovenproof dish.

Place a layer of the lasagne sheets over the base of the dish. Cover with a thin layer of bolognese sauce and top with another layer of lasagne sheets. Continue to layer the lasagne and the sauce – there should be enough for five layers of each. Top with the white sauce and sprinkle with the parmesan. Bake for 35–40 minutes, or until golden and bubbling. Allow to stand for 10 minutes before serving.

You can make and cook lasagne ahead of time and reheat in a 180°C (350°F, Gas Mark 4) oven for 15–20 minutes.

Serves 6

lemon cake.

185 g (6 oz) unsalted butter, softened

³/₄ cup caster (superfine) sugar

1 tablespoon finely grated lemon zest

3 eggs, lightly beaten

1¹/₂ cups self-raising (self-rising) flour, sifted

¹/₂ cup sugar

¹/₄ cup lemon juice

Preheat the oven to 160°C (315°F, Gas Mark 2–3). Grease a 23 × 12 cm (9 × 5 in) loaf tin and line the base with baking paper.

In an electric mixer, beat the butter, caster sugar and lemon zest for 2–3 minutes, or until soft and well mixed. Gradually add the beaten eggs, alternating with a spoonful of the flour, mixing well after each addition. Fold in the remaining flour and mix gently until smooth.

Spoon the batter into the prepared loaf tin and smooth the surface. Bake for 50–60 minutes, or until golden and firm to the touch. A skewer inserted in the centre should come out clean. Turn out onto a wire rack.

Mix together the sugar and lemon juice until just combined, without letting the sugar dissolve. Quickly spoon the sugar mixture over the top of the warm cake. The juice will sink into the cake and the sugar will form a crunchy topping.

Serves 8

lemon curd.

Lemon curd makes a great filling for cakes or small tarts or a topping for ice-cream or pavlova. Alternatively, simply spread onto buttered bread, hot toast, scones or English muffins.

3 lemons	110 g (3½ oz) unsalted butter
220 g (7 oz) caster (superfine) sugar	3 eggs, lightly beaten

Wash and dry the lemons. Finely grate the zest of one of the lemons. Place the zest, along with the sugar and butter, in a small, heavy-based saucepan over very low heat. Stir with a wooden spoon until the butter has melted and the sugar has dissolved.

Squeeze the three lemons and strain the juice. Add the juice and beaten eggs to the saucepan. Continue to cook over low heat, stirring constantly, until the mixture is thick enough to coat the back of the spoon. Do not allow the mixture to boil.

Stir the mixture well, pour into clean screw-top jars and seal. Allow to cool to room temperature before storing in the refrigerator for up to 1 month.

Lemon curd requires slow cooking and constant stirring, so don't rush the process by increasing the heat.

To make lime curd, substitute the lemon zest with the zest of 2 limes, and the lemon juice with the juice of 5 medium-sized limes.

To make orange curd, substitute the lemon zest with 1 tablespoon of finely grated orange zest, and the lemon juice with the juice of 2 medium-sized oranges.

To make passionfruit curd, substitute the lemon juice with the strained pulp of 8 passionfruit and the unstrained pulp of 2 passionfruit.

Makes 1½ cups

lemon delicious pudding.

This simple dessert consists of a rich, creamy lemon base topped
with a light golden sponge.

60 g (2 oz) unsalted butter, softened

³/₄ cup sugar

3 eggs, separated

2 teaspoons finely grated lemon zest

¹/₄ cup self-raising (self-rising) flour

³/₄ cup milk

¹/₃ cup lemon juice

Preheat the oven to 180°C (350°F, Gas Mark 4). Grease a deep 5-cup-capacity soufflé dish.

In an electric mixer, beat the butter, sugar, egg yolks and lemon zest until light and fluffy. Alternately fold in the flour and mix through the milk to make a smooth batter. Stir in the lemon juice. The batter may look like it has separated at this stage, but this is fine.

In a separate clean bowl, whisk the egg whites until firm. Gently fold the whites into the batter.

Pour the batter into the prepared dish. Place the dish in a large baking tin and fill the tin with enough boiling water to come a third of the way up the sides of the dish. Carefully transfer to the oven and bake for 50–55 minutes, or until the top is golden and risen. Dust with icing (confectioners') sugar and serve with cream.

*This pudding may also be cooked in six individual dishes, which take about
30 minutes to cook.*

Lime zest and juice can be substituted for the lemon, if you prefer.

Serves 6

lemon tart.

1 quantity sweet shortcrust pastry
(see page 146)
4 eggs
2 egg yolks

1 cup caster (superfine) sugar
2 tablespoons finely grated lemon zest
1$\frac{1}{4}$ cups lemon juice
$\frac{1}{2}$ cup cream

Prepare the pastry according to the instructions on page 146. Chill the pastry for at least 30 minutes before using.

Lightly grease a 25 cm (10 in) loose-based tart tin. Roll out the pastry between two sheets of baking paper so that it is large enough to fit the tart tin. Line the tin with the pastry, leaving a little pastry overhanging the tin. Refrigerate for 15 minutes.

Preheat the oven to 200°C (400°F, Gas Mark 6).

Line the pastry case with baking paper. Half-fill the pastry case with pie weights, uncooked dried beans or rice, and bake for 12 minutes. Remove the weights and baking paper, return the tin to the oven and cook for a further 10–15 minutes, or until the pastry is dry and lightly coloured. Set aside to cool. If the pastry case has any holes, plug them with a little uncooked pastry. With a sharp knife, cut off the overhanging pastry.

Reduce the oven temperature to 150°C (300°F, Gas Mark 2).

Whisk together the whole eggs, egg yolks and sugar until well combined. Whisk in the lemon zest and juice. Stir through the cream. Place the tart tin on a flat oven tray. Pour the egg and lemon mixture into the pastry case, filling almost to the top of the tart shell. Bake for 35–40 minutes, or until it is just set – the centre should wobble a little. The tart will firm up as it cools. Allow to cool for at least 1 hour before serving. Serve dusted with icing (confectioners') sugar.

Serves 8

lemonade.

Pop six extra lemons into your basket next time you go shopping.
Homemade lemonade is worth making, not only for its simplicity but
because of its ability to refresh and revive. The following recipe gives you
a concentrated base. Pour a little into a glass or jug, add ice and top up
with still or sparkling water to taste.

1½ cups sugar | 6 lemons

Place the sugar and 1½ cups of water in a small saucepan. Finely grate the zest of two of
the lemons and add this to the saucepan. Bring the mixture to the boil, stirring constantly.
Simmer for 5 minutes, or until the sugar has dissolved.

Squeeze the juice of all six lemons and add to the saucepan. Allow to cool.

Strain the mixture into a bottle, seal and store in the refrigerator for up to 5 days.
Dilute as required.

Choose ripe, bright yellow lemons that feel heavy for their size.
Add some freshly chopped mint leaves as a tasty variation.
Try this syrup with a dash of gin or vodka and diluted with soda or tonic water.

Makes 3 cups concentrated syrup

marinated olives.

500 g (1 lb) black or green olives

3 cloves garlic, finely sliced

1 large red chilli, seeded
   and finely chopped

2 teaspoons finely grated lemon zest

2 teaspoons chopped rosemary

3 sprigs thyme

2 bay leaves

olive oil, to cover

In a mixing bowl, combine the olives, garlic, chilli, lemon zest, rosemary, thyme and bay leaves, then spoon into a large glass jar. Add enough olive oil to cover the olives. Seal the jar and tap gently to dislodge any air bubbles.

Marinate in the refrigerator for 1–2 weeks before eating.

You can use many other flavour combinations for this versatile dish. Grated orange zest, basil leaves or anchovies are just a few other ingredients that work well. Vary the recipe above with one or more of these ingredients.

mashed potato.

1 kg (2 lb) floury potatoes, peeled and cut
    into chunks
1 cup milk

100 g (3½ oz) butter, cubed
salt and freshly ground black pepper

Place the potato pieces in a large saucepan of salted water. Bring to the boil and cook for 20–25 minutes, or until tender. Drain and return the potatoes to the saucepan. Cook over low heat for 1–2 minutes to remove any remaining moisture.

Meanwhile, heat the milk in a small saucepan over medium heat.

Mash the potatoes with the butter and ¾ cup of the hot milk until smooth. Beat well with a wooden spoon to fluff up the potato, adding a little more milk if needed. The mash should be soft and fluffy. Season to taste with salt and freshly ground black pepper.

The best mashed potato is made from varieties that are high in starch. Choose varieties such as bison, coliban, kennebec, sebago or spunta.

If you like a coarse texture to your mash, use a potato masher. Or for a really light, fluffy mash, push the potatoes through a mouli or potato ricer.

Try adding other vegetables, such as parsnip, celeriac or sweet potato (garnet yam), to the mash.

Add some gruyère cheese or pesto for a variation on standard mashed potato.

Serves 4–6

mayonnaise.

Mayonnaise is simple to make at home. I mix it by hand with a wire whisk, rather than whizzing it in the food processor, because I prefer the silky texture of a handmade mayonnaise.

2 egg yolks
1 teaspoon Dijon mustard
1 tablespoon lemon juice
salt

$^1/_4$ cup olive oil
$^3/_4$ cup vegetable oil
freshly ground black pepper

Place the egg yolks, mustard, lemon juice and a pinch of salt into a small bowl and whisk until smooth.

Combine the olive oil and vegetable oil in a jug. Pour it very slowly, drop by drop, into the egg mixture, whisking constantly. As the mixture thickens, start adding the oil in a steady stream. Continue until all the oil has been incorporated and the mixture is thick. Season to taste with salt and freshly ground black pepper. Taste and add a little more lemon juice if desired. The mixture can be thinned with boiling water, if necessary.

It's a good idea to stand the mixing bowl on a damp cloth while you're making mayonnaise. This prevents it from moving as you whisk.

The mixture may separate if the oil has been added too quickly. To remedy this, simply whisk up another egg yolk and gradually whisk this through the separated mixture in small amounts.

Mayonnaise can easily be flavoured. Chopped fresh herbs, garlic, anchovies, lemon zest, capers or chilli are just a few suggestions.

Makes $1^1/_2$ cups

meatballs.

1 thick slice Italian-style bread

milk, to soak

650 g (1 lb 5 oz) minced (ground) veal

2 cloves garlic, finely chopped

1/3 cup freshly grated parmesan

2 tablespoons chopped flat-leaf parsley

1 tablespoon chopped oregano

1 teaspoon finely grated lemon zest

1 large egg, lightly beaten

salt and freshly ground black pepper

plain (all-purpose) flour, to coat

2–3 tablespoons olive oil

1 × 400 g (13 oz) can crushed tomatoes

2 cloves garlic, peeled, extra

200 g (6½ oz) mozzarella, sliced or grated

chopped flat-leaf parsley, extra, to garnish

Remove the crust from the bread, break the bread into pieces and soak in a little milk. Squeeze dry, crumble and place in a large bowl. Add the minced veal, garlic, parmesan, parsley, oregano, lemon zest and beaten egg, and mix well. Season with plenty of salt and freshly ground black pepper. To check the seasoning, fry a small amount of the mixture until cooked through, and taste it. Adjust the seasoning to taste.

Shape the mixture into balls 5 cm (2 in) in diameter. Roll them in flour and shake off any excess.

Heat the oil in a large frying pan over medium heat. Add the meatballs and cook, turning, until brown all over. Remove and drain on kitchen paper.

Add the crushed tomatoes and whole garlic cloves to the frying pan. Bring to the boil, reduce the heat and simmer gently for 5 minutes. Return the meatballs to the pan and cook, turning them occasionally, for 5 minutes.

Preheat the oven to 180°C (350°F, Gas Mark 4).

Transfer the meatballs and sauce to an ovenproof dish. Top with the mozzarella and bake for 20 minutes. Sprinkle with the extra chopped parsley and serve with crusty bread to mop up the juices.

Serves 4–6

minestrone.

2 tablespoons olive oil

3 rashers bacon or pancetta, chopped

2 brown onions, chopped

1 leek, sliced

1 carrot, chopped

2 sticks celery, chopped

1 clove garlic, crushed

2 zucchini (courgettes), diced

400 g (13 oz) can crushed tomatoes

1.5 litres (48 fl oz) chicken stock
    (see page 36)

2 cups shredded spinach leaves

120 g (4 oz) small pasta shapes,
    such as orzo

400 g (13 oz) can cannellini beans, rinsed
    and drained

2 tablespoons chopped flat-leaf parsley
    or basil

salt and freshly ground black pepper

extra-virgin olive oil, to serve

freshly grated parmesan, to serve

Heat the oil in a large saucepan over low heat. Add the bacon or pancetta and cook, stirring, for 2 minutes. Add the onion, leek, carrot, celery and garlic. Cook, stirring, for 7–8 minutes, or until softened. This mixture gives the soup its flavour base.

Add the zucchini and crushed tomatoes to the saucepan. Cook, stirring, for 2 minutes. Add the chicken stock and 2 cups of water. Bring to the boil. Skim off any scum, reduce the heat and simmer gently for 30 minutes.

Add the spinach and pasta. Simmer for 20 minutes, stirring occasionally.

Add the cannellini beans and parsley. Add extra water or stock if there is not enough liquid, but remember, this is a thick soup. Season to taste with salt and freshly ground black pepper. Continue to cook for a further 10 minutes.

Ladle the soup into bowls, drizzle with extra-virgin olive oil and sprinkle with freshly grated parmesan.

Serves 4–6

muffins.

Muffins are fast, easy and infinitely variable.

2¼ cups plain (all-purpose) flour

2 teaspoons baking powder

½ teaspoon bicarbonate of soda
  (sodium bicarbonate)

salt

300 ml (9½ fl oz) buttermilk

2 eggs

1 teaspoon vanilla essence

¾ cup lightly packed brown sugar

125 g (4 oz) unsalted butter, melted

Preheat the oven to 190°C (375°F, Gas Mark 5). Grease a 12-cup muffin tin or line with paper patty cases.

Sift the flour, baking powder, bicarbonate of soda and a pinch of salt into a mixing bowl and make a well in the centre.

Whisk together the buttermilk, eggs, vanilla, sugar and melted butter. Pour the egg mixture into the well in the flour mixture and stir until the ingredients are just combined. Do not over-mix – the batter should not be smooth.

Divide the mixture evenly between the muffin cups. Bake for 20–25 minutes, or until the tops are golden and a skewer inserted into the centre of a muffin comes out clean. Allow to cool in the tin for 5 minutes before turning out onto a wire rack. Muffins are delicious served warm.

If you can't find buttermilk, use 150 ml (4½ fl oz) of natural yoghurt mixed with 150 ml (4½ fl oz) of milk.

To make blueberry muffins, fold 200 g (6½ oz) of fresh or frozen blueberries into the batter.

To make pecan muffins, fold in ¾ cup of chopped pecans. Sprinkle the top of each muffin with a little ground cinnamon and extra chopped nuts before baking.

Makes 12

mussels.

Mussels are perfect for a simple, fast and easy supper. For two people you will need 1–1.25 kg (2–2½ lb) of fresh mussels. Choose mussels that have perfect shells and that close firmly after they've been given a good tap. Soak the mussels in fresh water for 15 minutes, and then pull off their beards with a sharp tug.

2 tablespoons olive oil
1 onion, chopped
2 cloves garlic, crushed
1 tablespoon chopped flat-leaf parsley
1 cup white wine

¼ cup cream
1.25 kg (2½ lb) fresh mussels,
    cleaned and debearded
salt and freshly ground black pepper
chopped flat-leaf parsley, extra, to serve

Place a large saucepan or wok over medium heat. Add the oil, onion, garlic, parsley, wine and cream. Bring to the boil and simmer for 5 minutes. Add the mussels and increase the heat to high. Cover with a tight-fitting lid and cook for 3 minutes, giving the pan an occasional shake to help the mussels release their flavour.

Uncover and stir well. As the mussels open, transfer them to two deep serving bowls. Discard any that haven't opened after 5 minutes. Boil the broth for 2 minutes, season to taste with salt and freshly ground black pepper, and then strain over the mussels. Discard the solids. Sprinkle the mussels with the extra chopped parsley and serve immediately. Serve with crusty bread to mop up the delicious creamy broth.

Mussels are at their best from midwinter to the end of summer.

Serves 2

pancakes.

1 cup plain (all-purpose) flour
salt
2 tablespoons caster (superfine)
    sugar (optional)

2 eggs, lightly beaten
1 cup milk
30 g (1 oz) butter, melted

Sift the flour and a pinch of salt into a bowl. Stir in the caster sugar if you wish to make sweet pancakes. Make a well in the centre.

In a separate bowl, combine the beaten eggs, milk and melted butter. Pour the wet ingredients into the dry ingredients and mix until a smooth batter forms.

Grease a small non-stick frying pan and preheat over moderate heat for 1 minute.

Ladle the batter into the pan and cook for about 1 minute, or until bubbles appear on the pancake and the underside is golden. Using a spatula or fish slice, flip the pancake and cook for a further 45–60 seconds before turning out.

The pancake batter can be made ahead of time and left to rest for up to 2 hours.

Serve sweet pancakes with maple syrup, or try a squeeze of lemon juice and a sprinkling of sugar.

For savoury pancakes, fill with ratatouille or mushrooms cooked in a little cream.

A little grated zucchini (courgettes), chopped fresh herbs or spring onions (scallions) added to the batter also make delicious variations.

Makes 6–8

pannacotta.

Pannacotta is a traditional creamy pudding from Piedmont in northern Italy. This rich and delicious version is flavoured with orange and vanilla.

½ cup milk
1 × 10 g sachet (3 teaspoons) powdered gelatine
600 ml (20 fl oz) cream

¾ cup caster (superfine) sugar
1 teaspoon finely grated orange zest
1 teaspoon vanilla essence

Lightly grease six ½-cup-capacity pudding moulds.

Pour the milk into a small bowl. Stir in the gelatine and set aside.

Place the cream, sugar, orange zest and vanilla in a saucepan. Slowly bring to the boil, stirring until the sugar dissolves. Remove from the heat, add the gelatine mixture and stir until the gelatine dissolves. Set aside to cool for 15 minutes.

Strain the mixture and pour into the prepared moulds. Refrigerate for at least 4 hours, or until set.

To serve, dip the outside of each mould in hot water for 10 seconds, run a sharp knife around the inside of each mould and invert onto a serving plate. Serve as is or with fresh seasonal fruit.

Pannacotta can be made ahead of time and stored, covered, in the fridge for up to 3 days.

Serves 6

pavlova.

Pavlova is often referred to as Australia's national dessert,
but nothing this good remains a secret for long.

4 egg whites	$^1/_2$ teaspoon vanilla essence
salt	2 teaspoons cornflour (cornstarch)
1 cup caster (superfine) sugar	whipped cream, to serve
1 teaspoon white vinegar	ripe seasonal fruit, to serve

Preheat the oven to 120°C (250°F, Gas Mark 1–2). Line a baking tray with baking paper. Draw a circle 20 cm (8 in) in diameter in the middle of the piece of baking paper.

Place the egg whites and a pinch of salt in a clean, dry bowl. Beat with an electric mixer until soft peaks form. Gradually add the sugar, beating well after each addition. Beat until the mixture is stiff and glossy. Fold in the vinegar, vanilla and cornflour.

Heap the mixture within the circle on the baking paper. Shape into a circle with a spatula, leaving the centre slightly hollowed. Cook for 1–1$^1/_2$ hours, or until crisp on the outside. Turn off the oven and allow to cool in the oven with the door ajar.

To serve, top with whipped cream and sliced seasonal fruit.

Traditionally, pavlova is served with strawberries and passionfruit, but any fruit will do.

The base of the pavlova may be made a few days ahead and stored in an airtight container until ready to use.

As a variation, make individual pavlovas and top with berries and a fruit purée or coulis (see raspberry coulis, page 124).

Serves 8

pea soup.

This is a simple and modern version of an old favourite – pea and ham soup. The ham bone is replaced with bacon and I use fresh or frozen peas instead of the traditional dried variety. This soup is delicious served hot or cold.

1 tablespoon olive oil

2 rashers bacon, roughly chopped

1 onion, roughly chopped

1 stick celery, roughly chopped

1 leek, sliced

1 litre (32 fl oz) chicken stock
    (see page 36) or vegetable stock

500 g (1 lb) fresh or frozen peas

1 tablespoon roughly chopped mint

salt and freshly ground black pepper

Heat the oil in a large saucepan over medium heat. Add the bacon and cook, stirring occasionally, for 2 minutes. Add the onion, celery and leek, and cook, stirring constantly, for 4–5 minutes, or until the vegetables are tender but have not browned. Add the stock and bring to the boil. Reduce the heat and simmer for 15 minutes. Add the peas, return to the boil and simmer for 10 minutes.

Remove from the heat and allow to cool a little. Purée the soup in batches in a blender or with a hand-held blender until smooth. Season to taste with salt and freshly ground black pepper. Serve garnished with mint.

For a vegetarian version of this soup, omit the bacon and use vegetable stock.

Serves 4

pecan pie.

1 quantity sweet shortcrust pastry
  (see page 146)
1¹/₂ cups pecans
100 g (3¹/₂ oz) unsalted butter, melted
¹/₂ cup golden syrup

¹/₂ cup lightly packed brown sugar
3 eggs
¹/₂ teaspoon mixed spice
finely grated zest and juice of 1 lemon

Prepare the pastry according to the instructions on page 146. Chill the pastry for at least 30 minutes before using.

Lightly grease a 25 cm (10 in) loose-based tart tin. Roll out the pastry between two sheets of baking paper so that it is large enough to fit the tart tin. Line the tin with the pastry, leaving a little pastry overhanging the tin. Refrigerate for 15 minutes.

Preheat the oven to 200°C (400°F, Gas Mark 6).

Line the pastry case with baking paper. Half-fill the pastry case with pie weights, uncooked dried beans or rice, and bake for 12 minutes. Remove the weights and baking paper, return the tin to the oven and cook for a further 10–15 minutes, or until the pastry is dry and lightly coloured. Set aside to cool. If the pastry case has any holes, plug them with a little uncooked pastry. With a sharp knife, cut off the overhanging pastry.

Reduce the oven temperature to 180°C (350°F, Gas Mark 4).

Roughly chop half the pecans and place them in a large mixing bowl. Add the melted butter, golden syrup, sugar, eggs, spice, lemon zest and juice and mix well. Pour the mixture into the pastry case and top with the remaining whole pecans.

Bake for 25–30 minutes, or until firm. Remove from the oven and allow to cool for at least 20 minutes before removing from the tin. Serve warm or cold with thick cream or ice-cream.

Serves 8–10

pesto.

Purists make pesto by hand in a mortar and pestle, but use a blender
or food processor for a simple and fast result.

⅓ cup pine nuts

2 cups basil leaves

⅓ cup freshly grated parmesan

3 cloves garlic, roughly chopped

1 cup extra-virgin olive oil

salt and freshly ground black pepper

Place the pine nuts, basil, parmesan and garlic in a food processor or blender and process
until the mixture is roughly chopped.

With the motor running, slowly add the olive oil in a thin stream, and process until
the mixture is smooth but retains some texture. It will remain a good green colour so long
as it is not over-processed. Season to taste with salt and freshly ground black pepper. Store
in a screw-top jar, cover with a thin film of oil, and keep in the fridge for up to 2 weeks.

*Pesto is delicious stirred though a bowl of pasta or gnocchi. A teaspoon added to a bowl
of vegetable soup is the perfect finishing touch.*

Always use a good-quality extra-virgin olive oil and freshly purchased pine nuts for pesto.

Makes 2 cups

pizza base.

Pizza dough is easy to make; it simply needs a little time to rise.

1 × 7 g (¼ oz) sachet (2 teaspoons)
    dry yeast
1 teaspoon sugar

2½ cups bread flour
salt
2 tablespoons olive oil

Dissolve the yeast and sugar in a small bowl with 200 ml (6½ fl oz) of tepid water. Stir well and set aside for 10 minutes, or until the mixture froths.

Place the flour and a pinch of salt in a large mixing bowl. Make a well in the centre and add the yeast mixture and olive oil. Mix until a firm dough forms.

Knead on a lightly floured surface for 5–7 minutes, or until smooth and elastic. Place in a clean, lightly oiled bowl, cover with a cloth or plastic wrap and leave in a warm place for 1–1½ hours, or until the dough has doubled in size.

Preheat the oven to 210°C (415°F, Gas Mark 6–7).

Punch down the dough with your fist to release the air. Divide into two or three equal portions and roll out or press to a thickness of 4–5 mm (¼ in). Transfer to lightly oiled pizza trays.

Top with your choice of toppings and cook for 15 minutes. Then slide the pizza off the tray onto the oven shelf and cook for a further 3–4 minutes, to crisp up the base.

A good pizza base should have a little bit of chew, so don't roll out the dough any thinner than 4 mm (¼ in).

Pizza bases can be made and frozen, uncooked, for 2–3 months.

Don't overload your pizzas with toppings – less is definitely more.

Makes three 23 cm (9 in) or two 30 cm (12 in) pizza bases

poached eggs.

salt

white wine vinegar

4 fresh eggs

Half-fill a deep frying pan or wide saucepan with water. Add a teaspoon of salt and a dash of white vinegar. Bring the water to a gentle boil.

Carefully break one egg into a small, shallow dish or saucer and gently slide the egg into the simmering water. Repeat with the remaining eggs.

Lower the heat until the water is barely moving, allowing the eggs to cook gently without breaking. Cook for 4–5 minutes, or until the whites are set. Remove the eggs with a slotted spoon and drain.

The most successful poached eggs are made from very fresh eggs.

If the white separates from the yolk, it means the egg was not fresh, or that the water was not simmering sufficiently when the egg was added.

Only cook four eggs at a time in one frying pan or saucepan.

Serves 4

poached pears.

6 firm, ripe pears

1 lemon, halved

$^{1}/_{2}$ cup sugar

1 cinnamon stick

Carefully peel the pears, leaving the stalks attached if possible. Squeeze the juice of half a lemon over the pears as you peel them to stop them browning.

Place the peeled pears in a large saucepan. Add enough water to just cover. Remove the pears and set aside.

Add the sugar and cinnamon stick to the saucepan. Peel the zest from the remaining lemon half and add the zest to the saucepan. Bring the mixture to the boil, stirring to dissolve the sugar. Return the pears to the saucepan. Bring to the boil again, then reduce the heat and simmer for 15–20 minutes, or until the pears are tender.

Transfer the pears to a large serving dish. Strain the syrup, discarding the cinnamon and lemon zest, and return to the boil over high heat. Simmer rapidly until it is reduced by half. Pour the syrup over the pears. Serve warm or cold with cream or yoghurt.

Poached pears and chocolate are a classic combination. Serve pears with the chocolate sauce given on page 45.

Replacing 1 cup of the poaching water with 1 cup of red wine makes a delicious variation.

Serves 6

poached salmon with salsa verde.

4 salmon fillets
salt and freshly ground black pepper

SALSA VERDE
1 thick slice Italian-style bread
milk, to soak
1 cup loosely packed flat-leaf parsley
15 basil leaves
1 tablespoon capers
2 anchovy fillets
1 clove garlic, chopped
$1/4$ cup olive oil

To make the salsa verde, remove the crust from the bread, break the bread into pieces and soak it in a little milk. Squeeze dry and set aside.

In a food processor or blender, process the parsley, basil, capers, anchovies and garlic until roughly chopped. Add the milk-soaked bread. With the machine running, gradually add the olive oil in a thin stream, and process until the sauce is thick and smooth. Season to taste with salt and freshly ground black pepper.

Lay a salmon fillet, skin-side down, on a sheet of foil. Season well with salt and freshly ground black pepper. Wrap the fillet tightly in the foil, making an airtight seal. Repeat with the remaining fillets.

Place the wrapped fillets in a large saucepan and cover completely with cold water. Bring to the boil over medium heat. Reduce the heat and simmer gently for 2 minutes.

Remove the parcels from the saucepan. Open each one and remove the skin from the fish. Serve the salmon with the salsa verde, plus steamed potatoes and a mixed green salad.

Serves 4

porridge.

2 cups rolled oats

salt

brown sugar, to serve

warm milk, to serve

Place the rolled oats and a pinch of salt in a medium-sized saucepan. Add 2 cups of water and set aside for 5–10 minutes. (This helps to soften the oats and makes the finished product smoother and creamier.)

Add an extra $2^{1}/_{2}$ cups of water to the saucepan. Place over medium heat and bring to the boil, stirring frequently. Reduce the heat to low and simmer for 10–12 minutes, stirring frequently, until the mixture is soft and creamy.

Serve sprinkled with brown sugar and a jug of warm milk.

For a creamier version, replace 1 cup of water with 1 cup of milk and cook as above.
Add $^{1}/_{2}$ cup of sultanas or a mixture of dried fruits to the dry oats before cooking.
A mashed ripe banana or a grated apple is delicious added to the porridge while cooking.

Serves 4

pot of tea.

Throw out your teabags and return to the ritual of a *real* cuppa made from tea leaves! Personal taste, the strength of the brand of tea and the size of the pot will determine how much tea to use. As a guide, start by adding 2–3 teaspoons of tea leaves for an average-sized two-person pot.

Fill a kettle with fresh cold water and bring to the boil. When the water has almost reached the boil, pour a little into your teapot, swirl it around and pour it out. Add 2–3 teaspoons of tea leaves to the pot.

When the water is boiling, fill the teapot with boiling water. Put on the lid and leave to brew for 3–5 minutes.

The pot may be topped up later with more boiling water if needed.

Experiment by trying different types of tea. Look out for a specialist tea shop.

Black tea varieties include Orange Pekoe, Darjeeling, Assam, and blended varieties like English Breakfast and Earl Grey. These teas are dried and fermented to produce a dark-coloured leaf.

Green tea is made from the same plant as black tea but is not fermented. If making green tea, use water that has not quite come to the boil.

Serve full-flavoured teas such as Assam or English Breakfast in the morning. Orange Pekoe and Darjeeling are lighter, more aromatic teas and are perfect for an afternoon cuppa.

Serves 2

potato gratin.

600 ml (20 fl oz) cream

1 bay leaf

salt and freshly ground black pepper

1.5 kg (3 lb) desiree potatoes, peeled

2 cloves garlic, finely chopped

Preheat the oven to 170°C (325°F, Gas Mark 3). Grease a large, shallow ovenproof dish.

Place the cream and bay leaf in a large saucepan and season with freshly ground black pepper. Slowly bring to the boil, then simmer gently for 10 minutes. Remove the bay leaf.

Slice the potatoes very thinly. Add the slices to the saucepan, stir well and return the mixture to the boil. Simmer for 2–3 minutes, stirring gently.

Spoon a third of the potato mixture into the prepared dish, sprinkle with salt, pepper and a little chopped garlic. Repeat until the dish is full. Cover with foil and cook for 1 hour. Remove the foil and cook for a further 15–20 minutes, or until the top is golden and bubbling and the potato is tender.

Serves 6

potato salad.

1 kg (2 lb) waxy potatoes, scrubbed
2–3 tablespoons chopped flat-leaf parsley,
    chives or mint
4 finely sliced spring onions (scallions)
$^1/_2$ small red (Spanish) onion, finely sliced
salt and freshly ground black pepper
6 slices prosciutto or bacon

DRESSING
$^1/_2$ cup olive oil
1 tablespoon Dijon mustard
2 tablespoons white wine vinegar

Cook the potatoes in a large saucepan of gently boiling salted water for 12–15 minutes, or until just tender. Drain and allow to cool slightly.

While the potatoes are still warm, cut them into 2 cm ($^3/_4$ in) pieces and place in a large bowl with the parsley, spring onions and red onion. Season well with salt and freshly ground black pepper.

Place the dressing ingredients in a screw-top jar and shake well to combine. Pour half the dressing over the warm potatoes and toss gently to coat the pieces, being careful not to break up the potato. Allow to stand until most of the dressing is absorbed.

Meanwhile, cook the prosciutto or bacon in a frying pan or under a hot griller (broiler) until crisp. Prosciutto should take 3–4 minutes, bacon 5–7 minutes. Allow to cool, then break into bite-sized pieces.

Gently stir half the prosciutto or bacon into the salad. Transfer to a serving dish, drizzle with the remaining dressing and sprinkle over the remaining prosciutto or bacon. Serve warm or at room temperature.

For best results, use waxy potatoes such as kipflers, desirees, pink eyes, bintje, chats or small new potatoes when available.

Serves 4–6

pumpkin soup.

2 tablespoons vegetable oil

1 large onion, chopped

1 carrot, chopped

1 clove garlic, chopped

2 potatoes, peeled and chopped

500 g (1 lb) peeled and chopped pumpkin

1.25 litres (40 fl oz) chicken stock
(see page 36)

salt and freshly ground black pepper

yoghurt or sour cream, to serve

Heat the oil in a large saucepan over medium heat. Add the onion, carrot, garlic, potato and pumpkin. Cook, stirring, for 5 minutes, or until the onion has softened.

Add the stock and bring to the boil. Cover and simmer for 25–30 minutes, or until the vegetables are tender.

Allow to cool a little, then purée the mixture in batches in a blender or with a hand-held blender.

Gently reheat the soup. Season to taste with salt and freshly ground black pepper. Serve garnished with a dollop of yoghurt.

For an Asian-inspired soup, cook the vegetables with 1 tablespoon of Thai red curry paste. Stir in ¹/₂ cup of coconut milk before serving.

Serves 4

raspberry coulis.

250 g (8 oz) fresh raspberries
¼ cup icing (confectioners') sugar, sifted
1 tablespoon lemon juice

1–2 tablespoons raspberry-flavoured
brandy or raspberry-flavoured
liqueur (optional)

Purée the raspberries, icing sugar and lemon juice in a blender or food processor. Stir in the alcohol, if using. Pass the sauce through a strainer to remove any seeds.

Taste and add extra lemon juice or sugar if needed.

This coulis is good served with ice-cream, fresh or cooked fruit, chocolate cake, bavarois, pannacotta or tarts.

Thawed, frozen berries work equally well.

Replace the raspberries with an equal quantity of strawberries, blackberries or blueberries for a different berry coulis.

To make a mango coulis, use the flesh of two large ripe mangoes and follow the recipe above.

Makes 1½ cups

ratatouille.

Although not traditional, this is my favourite way to make ratatouille.

2 tablespoons olive oil
1 onion, chopped
2 cloves garlic, chopped
2 zucchini (courgettes), sliced
1 eggplant (aubergine), diced
1 large red capsicum (bell pepper),
    seeded and chopped

1 × 400 g (13 oz) can chopped tomatoes
salt and freshly ground black pepper
2 tablespoons roughly chopped basil
1 tablespoon lemon juice
extra-virgin olive oil, to serve

Heat the olive oil in a large frying pan and fry the onion and garlic over medium heat for 10 minutes, or until soft. Add the zucchini, eggplant and capsicum and cook for a further 10 minutes, stirring occasionally. Stir in the tomatoes, cover and simmer, stirring occasionally, for 10 minutes.

Season with salt and freshly ground black pepper. Stir in the basil and lemon juice and remove from the heat.

Serve ratatouille hot or cold, drizzled with a little extra-virgin olive oil.

Ratatouille is delicious served with roast meat, or as a filling for vegetarian lasagne. It also makes a great pasta sauce.

Serves 4

rhubarb and apple crumble.

1 bunch rhubarb

4 apples, peeled, cored and chopped

³/₄ cup sugar

juice of 1 lemon

1 cup plain (all-purpose) flour

³/₄ cup lightly packed brown sugar

¹/₂ teaspoon ground ginger

125 g (4 oz) unsalted butter, chilled
  and diced

¹/₄ cup flaked almonds

Grease a 4-cup-capacity ovenproof dish.

Trim the rhubarb and cut the stems into 2.5 cm (1 in) lengths. Set aside.

Heat a frying pan or large saucepan over medium heat and add the apples, sugar and lemon juice. Cook, stirring, for 3–4 minutes, or until tender.

Add the chopped rhubarb and cook for 4–5 minutes, or until the rhubarb is tender but still holds its shape. The rhubarb will give off a lot of liquid.

Use a slotted spoon to transfer the cooked fruit to the prepared dish. Leave behind any liquid remaining in the frying pan. Allow the fruit to cool a little. Taste and add extra sugar if needed.

Preheat the oven to 180°C (350°F, Gas Mark 4).

With your fingertips, rub together the flour, brown sugar, ginger and butter until the mixture resembles breadcrumbs and starts to clump together. Stir through the flaked almonds.

Sprinkle the crumble mixture evenly over the fruit. Bake for 30 minutes, or until golden and bubbling. Serve with cream or ice-cream.

Look for rhubarb with crisp red stalks. The deeper the colour, the sweeter the flavour.
Be careful to trim away any leaves from the rhubarb, as they are poisonous.
Granny Smith or any new-season apples make a good choice for this crumble.

Serves 4–6

rice.

To make the perfect fluffy rice, use the absorption method. Choose
long-grain rice such as basmati that will separate into fluffy individual
grains when cooked. This makes a delicious accompaniment
to braised food, Indian dishes or roast meats.

1 cup long-grain rice | salt

Place 600 ml (19 fl oz) of water, the rice and $^1/_2$ teaspoon of salt in a large saucepan and
bring to the boil over high heat. Stir once, then reduce the heat to the lowest setting
and cover with a tight-fitting lid. Cook for 15 minutes. Check that all the water has been
absorbed. If not, cook for a further couple of minutes. Remove from the heat and allow to
rest, covered, for 5–10 minutes. Fluff the rice with a fork before serving.

Use $^1/_4$ cup of rice and 150 ml ($4^1/_2$ fl oz) of water per person.

*Don't be tempted to stir the rice while it cooks, as this releases the starch in the grain
and makes it sticky.*

Serve rice plain or tossed with herbs, spices or cooked vegetables.

Serves 4

rice pudding.

3 cups milk

1 cup cream

finely grated zest of 1 orange

3 cardamom pods

$^1/_2$ cup short-grain rice, pudding rice
or arborio rice

$^1/_3$ cup caster (superfine) sugar

Combine the milk, cream and orange zest in a medium-sized saucepan.

Remove the seeds from the cardamom pods and crush them with the back of a knife. Add the crushed seeds to the saucepan.

Bring the mixture to the boil over medium heat. Reduce the heat to low, add the rice and sugar, and stir well until the sugar has dissolved. Simmer, stirring frequently to prevent the rice from sticking, for 30–35 minutes, or until the rice is soft and creamy and the mixture has thickened. Remove from the heat, cover and set aside for 15 minutes. Spoon into a large serving dish or into individual decorative dishes. Serve warm or cold.

Short-grain or pudding rice is traditionally used for rice pudding because the starch breaks down easily as it is cooked, giving the pudding a delicious creamy texture.

It is important to stir the rice frequently as it cooks. This helps to release the starch in the grains as well as to prevent the rice sticking to the pan.

Rice pudding is delicious served as it is or accompanied with fresh berries, orange segments or poached stone fruit.

Serves 4–6

risotto.

1.25 litres (40 fl oz) chicken stock (see page 36) or vegetable stock
45 g (1½ oz) butter
1 onion, finely chopped

1½ cups arborio or Carnaroli rice
⅓ cup dry white wine
½ cup freshly grated parmesan

Bring the stock to a gentle simmer in a large saucepan.

Meanwhile, heat 30 g (1 oz) of the butter in a large, heavy-based saucepan. Add the onion and cook, stirring, over moderate heat for 5 minutes, or until soft. The onion should soften but not change colour. Add the rice to the onion and stir gently for 2 minutes to coat the grains with a little butter. Add the wine. Stir and allow most of the liquid to evaporate.

Add the simmering stock, a ladleful at a time, to the rice mixture. The first amount of stock added should just cover the rice. Allow the rice to absorb the liquid before more stock is added. Stir frequently, and add more stock as required. It will take 18–25 minutes to cook. Taste the rice for texture – it should be soft but still retain a little bite.

Remove from the heat and add the remaining 15 g (½ oz) of butter and the grated parmesan. Cover and allow to rest for 5 minutes before serving.

The grains should fall easily from a spoon, and the liquid thicken to a creamy consistency. If necessary, moisten the risotto with a little more stock just before serving.

You can add almost anything you like to risotto. Try different combinations of herbs, sautéed mushrooms, cooked vegetables, cooked meats and seafood. Add ingredients towards the end of cooking.

Don't be tempted to leave out the butter at the end. Called 'mantecare', this process of adding the butter softens and marries all the flavours.

The better the stock, the better the risotto. Try homemade stock, such as chicken stock (see page 36).

Serves 4

roast capsicum.

red capsicums (bell peppers) | olive oil

Preheat the oven to 190°C (375°F, Gas Mark 5).

Brush the capsicums with oil and place in a single layer in a baking tin. Place in the top half of the oven and roast, turning occasionally, for 25–30 minutes, or until the skin is blackened and bubbling. Remove and transfer to a large heatproof bowl. Cover with plastic wrap and set aside to cool.

When cool, quarter the capsicums, discard the seeds and juice, and peel off the skin.

Use within 2 days or store by placing the capsicum quarters in a screw-top jar and filling with enough olive oil to cover. Refrigerate for up to 2 weeks.

Roast capsicum makes a great addition to an antipasto platter. It is also delicious added to salads or a frittata or quiche.

Chopped fresh herbs or peeled garlic added to a jar of roast capsicum make delicious variations.

roast chicken.

1 medium-sized chicken

1 lemon, halved

5 cloves garlic, unpeeled

1 tablespoon olive oil

salt and freshly ground black pepper

½ cup white wine

1½ cups chicken stock (see page 36)
or water

Preheat the oven to 200°C (400°F, Gas Mark 6).

Rinse the chicken and pat dry with kitchen paper. Place in a baking tin, breast-side up, and squeeze the juice of half a lemon over the bird. Place the other lemon half inside the cavity, along with one of the garlic cloves. Scatter the remaining garlic in the tin.

Drizzle the oil over the breast of the chicken. Sprinkle generously with salt and freshly ground black pepper.

Roast for 65–70 minutes, basting the bird with the pan juices every 20 minutes. To test if the chicken is cooked, insert a sharp knife or skewer into the thigh cavity – the juice should run clear.

Transfer the roasted chicken to a serving dish and allow to rest for 10 minutes. Warm the serving plates in the oven for 2–3 minutes.

To make a sauce, pour off the fat from the baking tin. Place the baking tin over medium heat on the stove top and add the wine and chicken stock. Stir well with a wooden spoon and scrape any bits stuck to the bottom of the tin, incorporating them into the sauce. Bring to the boil and simmer until the sauce is reduced and slightly thickened. Season to taste with salt and freshly ground black pepper. Alternatively, make a gravy by following the directions on page 77.

Use a free-range, chemical-free chicken if available.
A size 16 chicken (1.6 kg, 3¼ lb) will feed four people.

Serves 4

roast leg of lamb.

3 cloves garlic, peeled

1 medium-sized leg lamb

6–8 sprigs rosemary

2 tablespoons olive oil

salt and freshly ground black pepper

assorted vegetables, peeled and chopped,
    to roast

Preheat the oven to 200°C (400°F, Gas Mark 6).

Cut each garlic clove into three slivers. With the point of a small sharp knife, make six to eight incisions in the lamb. Insert the garlic slivers and a small sprig of rosemary into each of the cuts.

Rub the skin of the lamb with 1 tablespoon of the oil. Season with salt and freshly ground black pepper.

Place the lamb in a large baking tin and surround with a selection of peeled and chopped vegetables. Drizzle the vegetables with the remaining oil. Roast the lamb for 65–75 minutes, basting occasionally with the pan juices.

Remove the lamb from the tin, cover with foil and allow to rest for 10 minutes before carving. Keep the vegetables warm until ready to serve.

To make gravy, refer to the instructions on page 77.

Slice the lamb into medium–thick slices, serve with vegetables and accompany with gravy and mint sauce, if desired. If you have someone who is an expert carver, a roast leg of lamb looks magnificent presented at the table on a large platter surrounded by vegetables.

Carrots, potatoes, Jerusalem artichokes, parsnips, swedes, baby brown onions and chunks of sweet potato (garnet yam) are all delicious roasted along with the lamb.

Serves 4–6

roast pork with crackling.

The best crackling comes from the hindquarters, so choose either a pork
leg or loin to roast. Ask your butcher to score the skin for you.

1 × 1.5 kg (3 lb) piece pork
salt and freshly ground black pepper
3 sprigs rosemary

6 cloves garlic, unpeeled
1 kg (2 lb) potatoes, peeled and
    cut into chunks

Preheat the oven to 220°C (425°F, Gas Mark 7).

Pat the pork dry with kitchen paper and rub the scored skin well with salt. Season with
freshly ground pepper.

Place the pork, skin-side up, in a baking tin and tuck the rosemary and garlic under-
neath. Roast for 20 minutes.

Reduce the heat to 180°C (350°F, Gas Mark 4) and continue to cook for 1 hour.

Add the potatoes to the baking tin and cook, turning occasionally, for a further 1 hour,
or until the potatoes are tender inside and crisp on the outside. To test if the meat is
cooked, insert a sharp knife or skewer into the centre – the juice should run clear. Remove
the pork, cut away the crackling and return it to the top shelf of the oven if it needs further
cooking. Cover the meat and potatoes with foil and set aside to rest for 10 minutes.

To make gravy, refer to the instructions on page 77.

To serve, carve the pork into slices and accompany with potatoes, crackling, gravy and
apple sauce.

*Calculate the cooking time for different pork cuts by allowing 30 minutes for every 500 g
(1 lb), plus an extra 30 minutes.*

Serves 4–6

roast potatoes.

A perfect roast potato is crisp on the outside and soft and fluffy
on the inside.

1 kg (2 lb) floury potatoes	salt
2–3 tablespoons olive oil	

Preheat the oven to 200°C (400°F, Gas Mark 6).

Peel and cut the potatoes into even-sized pieces. Cook in a large saucepan of boiling salted water for 8–10 minutes, or until just tender. Drain well and return to the saucepan. Shake well in the pan, or use a fork to roughen up the surfaces a bit. (Rough edges help the potatoes to become crisp.)

Pour the oil into a baking tin and place in the hot oven for 5 minutes. Remove, add the potatoes to the tin and stir to coat with the oil. Season well with salt.

Roast on the top shelf of the oven, turning occasionally, for 50–60 minutes, or until crisp and golden. Serve with your favourite roast meat.

Floury potato varieties such as desiree, King Edward, roseval, spunta, kipfler or bintje are best for roasting.

Potatoes absorb less fat and cook faster if placed in a hot baking tin with hot oil.

As a variation, add 3–4 unpeeled garlic cloves and 1 tablespoon of chopped rosemary 10 minutes before the end of the cooking time. Or try chopped bacon stirred into the potatoes 7–10 minutes before the end of the cooking time.

Serves 4–6

salt and pepper squid.

600 g (1¼ lb) cleaned and prepared squid or calamari tubes
½ cup plain (all-purpose) flour or rice flour
2 tablespoons sea salt
1 tablespoon freshly ground black pepper
1 teaspoon chilli powder
1 medium-sized red chilli, finely chopped
vegetable oil, to fry

Rinse the squid. Cut along each side of the body so it opens out flat. Dry well with kitchen paper. Score the skin with a sharp knife and cut into either 1 cm (½ in) wide strips or 5 cm (2 in) diamonds.

In a shallow dish, combine the flour, sea salt, pepper, chilli powder and chopped chilli. Dip the pieces of squid into the flour mixture and toss to coat. Shake off any excess.

Pour vegetable oil into a large frying pan or wok to a depth of 2 cm (¾ in). Heat the oil to 180°C (350°F) – a cube of bread dropped in the oil should brown in 15 seconds.

Cook the squid in batches in the hot oil for 1–2 minutes, or until golden. Remove with tongs or a slotted spoon and drain on crumpled kitchen paper. Taste and season with a little extra salt and pepper if necessary. This dish should taste salty and spicy.

Serve with lemon or lime wedges.

Replace half the ground black pepper with 2 teaspoons of ground Sichuan peppercorns for an interesting flavour variation.

A pinch of Chinese five-spice powder is good added to the salt and pepper mix.

Peeled uncooked prawns are also good prepared this way.

Serves 4

scones.

3⅓ cups self-raising (self-rising) flour

1 teaspoon baking powder

1 tablespoon caster (superfine) sugar

½ teaspoon salt

60 g (2 oz) unsalted butter, chilled
    and diced

1 cup milk

2 teaspoons lemon juice

1 egg, beaten

milk, extra, for brushing

Preheat the oven to 200°C (400°F, Gas Mark 6). Line an oven tray with baking paper.

Sift the flour and baking powder into a large mixing bowl. Stir in the sugar and salt. Add the butter and, using your fingertips, rub the butter into the flour until it resembles fine breadcrumbs.

Mix together the milk and lemon juice – the mixture will curdle slightly. Add the beaten egg and pour into the flour mixture. Mix gently just until a dough forms – be careful not to overwork the dough. Gather into a rough ball shape, turn out onto a lightly floured surface and knead very lightly. The dough should feel slightly wet and sticky.

Flatten out the dough to a thickness of 3 cm (1¼ in) and cut out rounds with a cookie cutter. Place the rounds on the prepared oven tray 2.5 cm (1 in) apart and brush the tops with a little milk. Bake for 10–12 minutes, or until risen and golden.

Remove from the tray and wrap the scones in a clean tea towel to keep them warm and soft. Serve warm with jam, butter or cream.

To make fruit scones, add ½ cup of sultanas and some chopped orange zest.

To make cheese scones, omit the sugar and sift ½ teaspoon of dry mustard with the flour. After rubbing in the butter, stir ¾ cup of grated cheddar into the mixture and proceed with the recipe.

Makes 12

scrambled eggs.

To make perfect scrambled eggs, you need to cook the eggs
very slowly. The best way to achieve this is to cook them in a bowl
placed over a saucepan of simmering water. This method takes longer,
but the result is worth the effort.

6 eggs

1 tablespoon cream

salt and freshly ground black pepper

10 g (¼ oz) butter

Gently whisk the eggs with the cream and a pinch of salt and freshly ground black pepper
in a small heatproof mixing bowl.

Place the bowl over a saucepan of gently simmering water, making sure the bottom of
the bowl does not touch the water. Cook, turning the mixture occasionally with a large
metal spoon, until the egg thickens. As the egg thickens and begins to scramble, add the
butter. Season to taste with more salt and freshly ground black pepper. Serve on hot,
buttered toast.

Chopped chives or chervil are delicious folded into the mixture just before serving.
Dress up scrambled eggs with some smoked salmon and a glass of bubbly on the side.

Serves 2

seafood chowder.

2 tablespoons olive oil

1 onion, sliced

4 medium-sized potatoes,
    peeled and diced

2 tablespoons plain (all-purpose) flour

1.25 litres (40 fl oz) fish stock or
    vegetable stock

½ cup dry white wine

1 bay leaf

3 sprigs thyme

500 g (1 lb) firm white fish fillets

250 g (8 oz) smoked fish (haddock
    or cod) fillets

500 g (1 lb) medium-sized uncooked
    prawns (shrimp), peeled and deveined

1 cup cream or milk

salt and freshly ground black pepper

2 tablespoons chopped flat-leaf parsley
    or chervil

Heat the oil in a large saucepan, add the onion and potatoes and cook gently, without browning, until the onion is soft and translucent. Sprinkle over the flour and cook, stirring, for 1 minute.

Add the stock, wine, bay leaf and thyme and stir until smooth. Bring to the boil, reduce the heat and simmer for 10–15 minutes, or until the potatoes are soft. Remove the bay leaf and thyme.

Skin the white fish fillets and cut into bite-sized chunks. Break the smoked fish into bite-sized pieces. Add the fish and prawns to the saucepan and simmer for 3–4 minutes, or until the fish is opaque and the prawns have turned pink.

Stir in the cream or milk and heat slowly without bringing to the boil. Season well with salt and freshly ground black pepper. Sprinkle over the parsley or chervil and serve.

Serves 6

shepherd's pie.

2 tablespoons vegetable oil

2 onions, chopped

750 g (1½ lb) minced (ground) lamb

2 tablespoons plain (all-purpose) flour

1 cup beef stock

2 tablespoons tomato paste

2 teaspoons Worcestershire sauce

2 bay leaves

1 teaspoon fresh thyme, fresh marjoram
    or dried rosemary leaves

salt and freshly ground black pepper

750 g (1½ lb) floury potatoes, peeled

60 g (2 oz) butter

¼ cup milk

20 g (¾ oz) butter, extra

pinch of cayenne pepper

Heat 1 tablespoon of the oil in a frying pan over medium heat and cook the onions for 4–5 minutes, or until soft and golden. Remove and set aside.

Heat the remaining 1 tablespoon of oil in the same frying pan and add the lamb. Cook over medium heat, stirring occasionally, for 7 minutes. Use a fork to break up any lumps. Stir in the flour and cook for 1 minute. Remove from the heat and add the stock, stirring until blended. Return to the heat and bring to the boil, stirring continuously, until thickened. Add the cooked onions, tomato paste, Worcestershire sauce, bay leaves and thyme, marjoram or rosemary. Season to taste with salt and freshly ground black pepper. Set aside to cool.

Meanwhile, cut the potatoes into chunks and cook in a large saucepan of boiling salted water for 15–20 minutes, or until tender. Drain well and mash with the butter and milk until smooth. Season well with salt and freshly ground black pepper.

Preheat the oven to 180°C (350°F, Gas Mark 4).

Transfer the meat mixture to a large ovenproof dish. Spoon over the mashed potato and fluff up with a fork. Dot with the extra butter and sprinkle with the cayenne pepper. Bake for 30–35 minutes, or until golden and bubbling. Serve at the table directly from the dish. Accompany with steamed green beans or spinach.

Serves 4–6

shortbread.

250 g (8 oz) unsalted butter, softened

½ cup caster (superfine) sugar

2 cups plain (all-purpose) flour

½ cup rice flour

Preheat the oven to 150°C (300°F, Gas Mark 2). Line two oven trays with baking paper.

Beat the butter in a bowl with a wooden spoon until soft and smooth. Add the sugar, plain flour and rice flour and work the mixture with the spoon until blended.

Knead the dough lightly on a floured surface to form a firm dough, then chill for 20 minutes.

Divide the dough into two portions and roll out each between two sheets of baking paper to a thickness of 5–7 mm (¼–⅓ in). Cut the dough into shapes with cookie cutters. Place the shapes onto the prepared oven trays and bake for 15–20 minutes, or until pale and dry. Alternatively, roll out each portion of dough to form a circle 18 cm (7 in) in diameter. Mark each circle into wedges with a knife, prick the surface several times with a fork, sprinkle with a little extra sugar and bake for 35–40 minutes, or until pale and dry. Store shortbread in an airtight container for up to 1 week.

Shortbread should be dry with a melt-in-the-mouth texture.

Rice flour gives the shortbread a wonderful grainy texture.

As a variation, add a little grated or finely chopped citrus zest to the dough.

Makes 35–40 biscuits or 2 large rounds

shortcrust pastry.

Shortcrust pastry is easy to make and is suitable for tarts, pies or quiches.
Sweet shortcrust is enriched with a little sugar and a beaten egg, which
makes it perfect for sweet tarts (see recipe variation below).

2 cups plain (all-purpose) flour

salt

125 g (4 oz) butter, chilled and diced

3–4 tablespoons chilled water

Sift the flour and a pinch of salt into a large bowl. Rub the butter into the flour mixture
with your fingertips until it resembles fine breadcrumbs. (As you rub the butter into the
flour, lift it up high and let it fall back into the bowl.) Alternatively, pulse the mixture in
a food processor until the mixture resembles fine breadcrumbs.

Make a well in the centre, add the chilled water and mix with a flat-bladed knife, using
a cutting action rather than a stirring action, until the mixture comes together in beads.
Add a little extra water if needed to bring the dough together.

Gather the dough, press gently together into a ball and flatten slightly into a disc.
Wrap in plastic wrap and refrigerate for 30 minutes before using.

Homemade shortcrust pastry can be covered in plastic wrap and stored in the fridge for
2–3 days, or frozen for 2–3 months.

*To make a sweet shortcrust pastry, add 1 tablespoon of icing (confectioners') sugar to the
flour. Add 1 beaten egg yolk and only 2–3 tablespoons of chilled water to the mixture and
then follow the basic recipe.*

*The easiest way to roll out the pastry is to place the ball of dough between two sheets
of baking paper and use a large rolling pin. The paper prevents the dough sticking to the
surface and makes it easier to handle.*

Makes enough for a 20 cm (8 in) pie

slow-roasted tomatoes.

8 Roma (egg) tomatoes

olive oil

2 teaspoons thyme leaves

salt and freshly ground black pepper

Preheat the oven to 140°C (275°F, Gas Mark 1) and lightly grease an oven tray.

Cut the tomatoes in half lengthways and place, cut-side up, on the prepared oven tray. Drizzle each tomato half lightly with olive oil, then sprinkle evenly with thyme, salt and freshly grated black pepper.

Roast for $1^1/_2$–2 hours, or until the tomatoes are lightly dried and darkened, but still retain some moisture. Use in salads, as part of sandwich fillings, or tossed through cooked pasta. To store, cover completely with olive oil in a screw-top jar and keep in the refrigerator up to 2 weeks.

Makes 16

spaghetti with garlic, chilli and oil.

This is the simplest and speediest of all pasta dishes. Olive oil is infused with garlic and chilli, which is then stirred into hot pasta. This dish fills the kitchen with the heady aroma of garlic.

400 g (13 oz) dried spaghetti
$^{1}/_{2}$ cup olive oil
4 cloves garlic, finely chopped

1–2 large red chillies, seeded
    and finely chopped
2 tablespoons chopped flat-leaf parsley
salt and freshly ground black pepper

Bring a large saucepan of salted water to the boil and add the spaghetti. Stir well and boil rapidly for 8 minutes, or until the spaghetti is al dente.

Meanwhile, combine the oil, garlic and chilli in a small saucepan. Cook over very low heat for 7–8 minutes to allow the oil to absorb the chilli and garlic flavours. The oil should barely simmer. The garlic should colour slightly, but don't allow it to burn.

Drain the cooked pasta and return it to the large saucepan over moderate heat. Pour over the oil mixture and add the parsley. Toss thoroughly with two forks to coat the pasta with the oil. Season with salt and freshly ground black pepper. Serve immediately.

Allow 100 g ($3^{1}/_{2}$ oz) of dried spaghetti per person.
You can vary this dish by using chopped basil or chopped rocket (arugula) in place of the parsley. A squeeze of lemon juice is also delicious.
If you like, serve with freshly grated parmesan.

Serves 4

spiced nuts.

350 g (11 oz) unsalted mixed nuts
2 tablespoons olive oil
1 tablespoon brown sugar
2 tablespoons sea salt

¼ teaspoon cayenne pepper
½ teaspoon ground turmeric
freshly ground black pepper (optional)

Combine all the ingredients in a mixing bowl. Add a little extra cayenne pepper and a grinding of black pepper if you prefer a spicier mix.

Place in a large frying pan and cook, stirring frequently, over moderate heat for 5–7 minutes, or until golden. Taste and season with a little extra salt if desired.

Allow to cool and serve in small bowls as a snack. Spiced nuts make a perfect accompaniment to a drink or two. Once completely cool, store the nuts in an airtight container for up to 1 week.

Make a mixture of your personal favourites. Try macadamias, pecans, cashews and Brazil nuts.

A tablespoon of toasted sesame seeds stirred through the mix makes a delicious addition.

Makes 2 cups

sponge cake.

6 eggs

¾ cup caster (superfine) sugar

1 teaspoon vanilla essence

1 cup plain (all-purpose) flour, sifted

½ cup self-raising (self-rising) flour, sifted

75 g (2½ oz) unsalted butter, melted and cooled

1 cup berry jam

1 cup cream

½ teaspoon vanilla extract

icing (confectioners') sugar, to dust

Preheat oven to 180°C (350°F, Gas Mark 4). Grease two 22 cm (8½ in) shallow round cake tins and line the base of each with baking paper.

Combine the eggs, sugar and vanilla in a large heatproof bowl. Place the bowl over a saucepan of gently simmering water, making sure the base of the bowl doesn't touch the water. Beat with an electric mixer for 6–7 minutes, or until pale, thick and doubled in bulk. Remove from the heat and continue to beat for 3 minutes.

Using a large metal spoon, gently fold in the sifted flours, followed by the cooled melted butter. Mix until just combined and there is no trace of white flour.

Spread the mixture evenly into the prepared tins and bake for 25–30 minutes, or until golden and firm to the touch. Leave to cool in the tins for 5 minutes, then turn out onto a wire rack to cool completely.

Spread the jam evenly over one of the cakes. Whip the cream and vanilla until soft peaks form, then spoon or pipe the cream over the jam. Top with the remaining cake. Dust with icing sugar.

It is important to fold in the flour and butter very gently. If you are too vigorous at this stage, you will lose a lot of volume in the egg mixture.

Serves 8

steak.

Choose a good cut of aged meat – either a New York cut, sirloin, T-bone, rump or fillet – about 2.5–3.5 cm (1–1½ in) thick. Allow about 200–250 g (6½–8 oz) per person. Have the butcher trim off the outer layer of fat.

1 × 200–250 g (6½–8 oz) steak
olive oil, to brush

freshly ground black pepper

Brush one side of the steak with oil and give it a good grinding of black pepper.

Preheat a heavy-based cast-iron frying pan, grill plate or barbecue to very hot.

Sear the steak, oil-side down first, cooking for the desired time (see below). Brush with more oil, give it a good grinding of black pepper, turn the steak over and cook the other side.

Remove from the heat, wrap in foil and allow to rest for 5–10 minutes before serving. Serve with herb butter or mustard and a crisp green salad.

For a rare steak, cook 2–3 minutes each side. For medium, cook 3–4 minutes each side. For well done, cook 3 minutes each side, then turn down the heat and cook for 8–10 minutes, turning once.

To make herb butter, beat 1 chopped clove of garlic and 2 tablespoons of chopped fresh herbs with 100 g (3½ oz) of softened butter until combined. Roll into a log shape, cover with plastic wrap and refrigerate until firm. Cut into slices and serve on top of a hot steak.

Serves 1

sticky date pudding.

175 g (6 oz) pitted dates, chopped

1 teaspoon bicarbonate of soda
   (sodium bicarbonate)

60 g (2 oz) unsalted butter, softened

3/4 cup caster (superfine) sugar

2 eggs, lightly beaten

1 1/2 cups self-raising (self-rising) flour

1/2 teaspoon vanilla essence

SAUCE

125 g (4 oz) unsalted butter, cubed

3/4 cup lightly packed brown sugar

200 ml (6 1/2 fl oz) cream

Preheat the oven to 180°C (350°F, Gas Mark 4). Grease an 18 cm (7 in) square cake tin and line the base and sides with baking paper.

Place the dates in a bowl. Add the bicarbonate of soda and pour over 300 ml (9 1/2 fl oz) of boiling water. Set aside.

Beat the softened butter and caster sugar until pale and fluffy. Add the beaten eggs, a bit at a time, beating well after each addition. Sift in the flour. Add the dates and their juice, then the vanilla. Mix well. This will be a wet mixture.

Pour into the prepared tin and bake for 35–45 minutes, or until risen and firm to touch. A skewer inserted in the centre should come out clean.

Meanwhile, make the sauce by placing the butter, brown sugar and cream in a small saucepan. Bring to the boil and simmer for 5 minutes.

Turn the pudding out of the tin and place on a baking tray. Pour one-third of the sauce over the pudding and return it to the oven for 5 minutes, or until golden and bubbling. This gives the pudding a delicious hot caramel topping.

Cut the pudding into squares and serve topped with the remaining sauce, plus cream or ice-cream.

Serves 6–8

strawberry fool.

Nothing could be simpler than this dessert – the perfect fool is just cream, fruit and sugar. Any crushed fruit can make a delicious fool, but soft fruits such as strawberries or raspberries are traditionally used.

250 g (8 oz) strawberries, hulled
2–3 tablespoons icing (confectioners') sugar

1 cup cream

Mash the strawberries with the icing sugar until soft and pulpy. (I prefer the slightly lumpy effect obtained by mashing the fruit and the sugar with a fork or potato masher; however, this can just as easily be pulsed in an electric blender.)

Whip the cream until soft peaks form. Stir the cream into the fruit mixture. Taste and add a little extra fruit if desired.

Pile into decorative glasses and chill. Serve accompanied with thin shortbread or wafers.

Although it doesn't dissolve as easily in the fruit, caster (superfine) sugar can be used in place of the icing sugar.

Equal quantities of strawberries and raspberries make a delicious combination.

Try making a fruit fool using the puréed flesh of 2 mangoes, or alternatively the pulp of 6 passionfruit and a squeeze of lime juice.

The addition of a tablespoon or two of plain yoghurt gives an interesting flavour, but you may need to add a little more sugar.

Serves 4

strawberry jam.

1.25 kg (2½ lb) sugar

1.5 kg (3 lb) strawberries, hulled

⅓ cup lemon juice

Preheat the oven to 140°C (275°F, Gas Mark 1).

Place the sugar in an ovenproof dish and warm for 10 minutes. Place clean jam jars in the oven to warm also. Put two saucers into the freezer to chill.

Place the strawberries, lemon juice, warm sugar and ½ cup of water into a large saucepan. Stir over low heat until the sugar has dissolved. Increase the heat and simmer gently for 20 minutes, stirring frequently. Skim off any scum that rises to surface.

Remove from the heat. Drop 1 teaspoon of jam on one of the chilled saucers and return to the freezer for 1 minute. If the jam forms a skin and wrinkles when pushed with a fingertip, it has reached setting point. If not, continue to cook the mixture, testing every 5 minutes, until the jam reaches setting point. Remove from the heat and allow to stand for 15 minutes before bottling.

Spoon the jam into the warmed jars and allow to cool. Seal, label and date the jars. Store in a cool, dark place for up to 12 months.

Makes 6 cups

sweet chilli sauce.

This versatile sauce goes well with chicken, seafood and meat. Although the recipe contains chillies, sugar is used to take the edge off the heat and give the sauce a pleasant and balanced taste.

3/4 cup sugar

1/2 cup white vinegar

1 teaspoon salt

4 cloves garlic, crushed

6 large red chillies, seeded and roughly chopped

1 tablespoon grated fresh ginger

1 teaspoon Thai fish sauce

Place the sugar, vinegar, salt and 1 cup of water in a small stainless-steel saucepan. Bring to the boil, stirring to dissolve the sugar, and simmer for 5 minutes.

Add the garlic, chillies and ginger to the saucepan. Simmer over medium heat, stirring frequently, for 15–20 minutes, or until reduced and thickened. Remove from the heat and stir through the fish sauce.

Pulse the mixture in a food processor or blender to produce a sauce with speckles of red chilli. Transfer to a clean, sterilised jar and seal. Serve at room temperature. The sauce can be stored in the refrigerator for up to 1 month.

Using large red chillies, which are milder than small ones, allows you to incorporate enough chilli to achieve a good red-coloured sauce. Add a small red chilli if you prefer the sauce a little hotter.

Makes 1 cup

thai beef salad.

Thai salads are a combination of opposing tastes and textures – crisp salad leaves, soft noodles and a sweet–sour sauce. Use these principles to create your own combinations.

500 g (1 lb) beef fillet or rump
85 g (3 oz) cellophane noodles
1 small cucumber, peeled and diced
250 g (8 oz) mixed salad leaves

DRESSING
2 tablespoons Thai fish sauce
2 tablespoons lime juice
1 tablespoon soy sauce
1 teaspoon vegetable oil
2 small red chillies, seeded
    and finely chopped
2 teaspoons soft brown sugar or palm sugar

Cook the beef in a hot frying pan or grill pan for 2–3 minutes each side, or until cooked to your liking. Allow to cool.

Place the cellophane noodles in a heatproof bowl and cover with boiling water. Leave for 6–7 minutes, or until soft. Drain well and cut into 3 cm (1 1/4 in) lengths.

Place the dressing ingredients in a screw-top jar and shake well to combine.

Slice the beef thinly.

To serve, mix together the cucumber and salad leaves and place on a large platter or in a large bowl. Top with the noodles and slices of beef. Pour over the dressing.

If time permits, brush the beef with a pounded mixture of 2 garlic cloves, 3 coriander roots, a squeeze of lime juice and 2 tablespoons of vegetable oil. Marinate for 20 minutes before cooking. The beef may be substituted with lamb fillets, chicken fillets or baby squid.

Serves 4

thai-style prawn broth.

1 kg (2 lb) uncooked medium-sized
    prawns (shrimp)
2 stems lemongrass, sliced
2 kaffir lime leaves, finely sliced
2 cloves garlic, chopped
1 teaspoon grated fresh ginger
2 tablespoons chopped coriander
    (cilantro) stems
2 large red chillies, seeded and sliced

1 litre (32 fl oz) fish stock or chicken stock
    (see page 36)
250 g (8 oz) fresh rice noodles
6 spring onions (scallions), sliced
1 tablespoon Thai fish sauce
2–3 tablespoons lime juice
2 cups bean sprouts
salt and freshly ground black pepper
    (optional)
$1/3$ cup fresh coriander (cilantro) leaves

Peel and devein the prawns, leaving the tails intact. Set aside.

Place the prawn heads and shells in a large saucepan with the lemongrass, lime leaves, garlic, ginger, coriander stems and half the chilli. Add the stock and 2 cups of water and bring to the boil. Reduce the heat and simmer for 15 minutes. Strain and discard the solids.

Return the broth to the saucepan and bring to the boil over medium heat. Add the noodles and simmer for 5 minutes, or until soft.

Add the prawns, spring onions, fish sauce, lime juice and the remaining chilli. Cook for 2 minutes, or until the prawns turn pink. Add the bean sprouts.

Taste the broth and add extra fish sauce, lime juice, salt or pepper as desired. Serve immediately, garnished with the coriander leaves.

Serves 4

tomato relish.

This relish is deliciously spicy and easy to make. I love it served alongside sausages, cold meats or cheese. A dollop on a cheese sandwich is perfect.

1 kg (2 lb) ripe tomatoes
1 large onion, finely chopped
2 cloves garlic, crushed
2 small red chillies, sliced
1 cup lightly packed brown sugar
1 cup red wine vinegar

$\frac{1}{3}$ cup olive oil
1 teaspoon ground ginger
1 teaspoon ground cumin
1 teaspoon curry powder
salt and freshly ground black pepper

Preheat the oven to 140°C (275°F, Gas Mark 1).

Place clean jam jars in the oven to warm.

Meanwhile, halve the tomatoes and remove the seeds. Roughly chop the tomatoes and place in a saucepan with the remaining ingredients except the salt and pepper. Bring to the boil, reduce the heat and simmer gently, stirring occasionally, for 50–60 minutes, or until the relish is thick, pulpy and jam-like. Season well with salt and freshly ground black pepper.

Pour the relish into warm jam jars and allow to cool. Seal when cold. Store in the fridge for 1 month.

Makes 3 cups

tomato sauce for pasta (pomodoro).

2 tablespoons olive oil

2 onions, chopped

3 cloves garlic, chopped

2 × 400 g (13 oz) cans chopped tomatoes

1 tablespoon sugar

2 tablespoons tomato paste

2 tablespoons finely chopped basil

Heat the oil in a large saucepan over medium heat and sauté the onions and garlic for 5 minutes. Add the tomatoes and sugar and bring to the boil. Reduce the heat and simmer gently, stirring occasionally, for 20 minutes, or until soft and pulpy.

Stir in the tomato paste and basil. Serve as is, or as a purée if you prefer a smoother consistency.

Instead of canned tomatoes you can use 1 kg (2 lb) of peeled, ripe tomatoes.

Serves 4

tomato soup.

Tomato soup is an all-time favourite – worthy of serving as a simple Sunday-night meal for family, or as a starter at a fine dinner party for friends.

2 tablespoons olive oil
1 onion, chopped
1 carrot, chopped
1 stick celery, chopped
2 cloves garlic, chopped
750 g (1½ lb) ripe tomatoes, quartered

1 × 400 g (13 oz) can chopped tomatoes
1 litre (32 fl oz) chicken stock (see page 36)
    or vegetable stock
salt and freshly ground black pepper
1 tablespoon chopped basil, to garnish
extra-virgin olive oil, to garnish

Heat the oil in a large saucepan. Sauté the onion, carrot, celery and garlic for 5 minutes, then add the fresh tomatoes and cook for 3–4 minutes.

Add the canned tomatoes, stock and 1 cup of water. Bring to the boil, reduce the heat and simmer for 30 minutes.

Remove from the heat and allow to cool a little. Purée the soup in batches in a blender or with a hand-held blender.

Season to taste with salt and freshly ground black pepper.

Serve hot, garnished with chopped basil and a drizzle of extra-virgin olive oil.

Use the best ripe red tomatoes you can find. If the tomatoes lack flavour, add 1 tablespoon of tomato paste.

For a richer version, serve drizzled with a little cream or a dollop of sour cream.

Serves 4

upside-down pear cake.

90 g (3 oz) unsalted butter, melted

1/2 cup raw sugar or demerera sugar

4 large ripe pears, peeled, cored
and quartered

125 g (4 oz) unsalted butter, extra

1/2 cup golden syrup

1 1/2 cups plain (all-purpose) flour

1 teaspoon bicarbonate of soda
(sodium bicarbonate)

2 teaspoons ground ginger

1 teaspoon mixed spice

salt

1 cup firmly packed brown sugar

1 cup buttermilk or milk

2 eggs, beaten

Preheat the oven to 180°C (350°F, Gas Mark 4). Lightly grease the sides of a 26 cm (10 1/2 in) springform cake tin.

Pour the melted butter into the cake tin and sprinkle over the raw sugar. Arrange the pear quarters, cut-side up, in the base of the cake tin.

Place the extra 125 g (4 oz) of butter and the golden syrup in a small saucepan. Stir over low heat until the butter has melted.

Sift the flour, bicarbonate of soda, ground ginger, mixed spice and a pinch of salt into a mixing bowl. Stir in the brown sugar. Add the milk and eggs and beat with a wooden spoon until smooth. Gradually add the warm butter and golden syrup mixture, stirring well until smooth.

Pour the batter over the pears in the cake tin. Bake for 60–70 minutes, or until a skewer inserted into the centre of the cake comes out clean. Leave to cool for 15 minutes before turning out onto a wire rack to cool completely.

Halved and cored plums, or peeled, cored and chopped apples, or sliced pineapple rings all make good substitutes for the pears.

Serves 8–10

vanilla bean ice-cream.

2 cups milk

1 vanilla bean

6 egg yolks

125 g (4 oz) caster (superfine) sugar

1 cup cream, lightly whipped

Pour the milk into a small saucepan.

Using a sharp knife, split the vanilla bean in half lengthways. Scrape out the seeds and add the pod and the seeds to the saucepan of milk. Bring the mixture to simmering point over low heat.

In a large mixing bowl, whisk together the egg yolks and sugar for 4–5 minutes, or until the sugar has dissolved and the mixture is thick and pale. Gently whisk the hot milk mixture, including the vanilla bean pod, into the yolk mixture.

Return this mixture to the saucepan and cook over low heat, stirring constantly with a wooden spoon, until the mixture thickens slightly and coats the back of the spoon. Do not allow the mixture to boil or it will curdle. Remove from the heat and strain into a bowl, discarding the bean pod. Set aside to cool.

When cold, whisk in the whipped cream. Churn in an ice-cream machine until firm.

Before serving, soften the ice-cream by placing in the fridge for 15 minutes.

Serves 4–6

vietnamese dipping sauce.

Few tables in southeast Asia are without a little dish of this Vietnamese
chilli dipping sauce known as nuoc cham. It is used as a dip for spring
rolls and crudités, and to add flavour and heat to noodle and rice dishes.
The flavour should be a balance of sweet, sour, salt, chilli and garlic.

¼ cup fish sauce

1 tablespoon white vinegar

2 tablespoons lime juice

2 teaspoons palm sugar or soft brown sugar

2 large red chillies, seeded and thinly sliced

2 cloves garlic, finely chopped

½ small carrot, coarsely grated (optional)

Combine the fish sauce, vinegar, lime juice and 1 tablespoon of water in a small bowl. Add
the sugar and stir to dissolve. Add the chillies and garlic. A coarsely grated carrot is often
added to give the sauce crunch. Stir well and serve immediately.

*As a variation, try adding 1–2 teaspoons of chopped fresh coriander (cilantro) leaves
or 1 sliced spring onion (scallion).*

*Remember, there are no fixed rules with this sauce. Taste as you go and adjust the balance
of flavours to suit you.*

*Nuoc cham is best made just prior to serving. If made ahead, the chilli flavour can often
dominate.*

Makes ¾ cup

vinaigrette.

A vinaigrette is simply a combination of oil and vinegar, held together
with a little Dijon mustard and seasoned with salt and pepper. The classic
proportion for a vinaigrette is one part vinegar (or an acidic juice
such as lemon juice) to three parts oil.

2 tablespoons vinegar or lemon juice

1 teaspoon Dijon mustard

$^1/_2$ cup olive oil

salt and freshly ground black pepper

Place the vinegar or lemon juice, mustard and olive oil in a screw-top jar. Season well with
salt and freshly ground black pepper. Put the lid on the jar and shake well to combine. The
vinaigrette will keep for 4–5 days in the fridge.

*Vary the types of oil and vinegar you use. When choosing the oil and vinegar, remember
they should complement each other. The rich texture and fruity taste of extra-virgin olive oil
is well balanced by balsamic vinegar, whereas nut oils are good teamed with fruit vinegars.
Chilli- or herb-flavoured oils are balanced by the use of wine vinegars or lemon juice.*

*The oil and vinegar will separate on standing, so store in a screw-top jar and shake
well just before adding to a salad.*

*Use crushed garlic, chopped fresh chilli or chopped fresh herbs to add variety to
the vinaigrette.*

Makes $^1/_2$ cup

watermelon and lime granita.

A granita is a frozen grainy water ice made from lightly sweetened fruit syrup. It's delicious on a hot summer's day.

½ cup sugar

2 cups puréed watermelon flesh

2 tablespoons lime juice

Combine the sugar and ½ cup of water in a small saucepan. Bring to the boil over medium heat, stirring to dissolve the sugar. Allow to cool.

Combine the watermelon purée and the lime juice with the cool syrup. Pour into a shallow container, cover and freeze for 1 hour, or until the purée around the edge of the tray is frozen. Break up the crystals with a fork using a scraping action. Return to the freezer and repeat the scraping procedure every 45 minutes, or until you have a glistening mass of smooth ice crystals. This can take 2–3 hours.

Ideally the granita should be eaten at once, but it may be poured into a storage container, covered with greaseproof paper and returned to the freezer. To serve, soften the mixture in the fridge for 10–15 minutes, then stir again with a fork to break up the ice crystals. Serve within 1–2 days, in tall glasses with long spoons.

If you have stored the granita overnight, you will need to soften, scrape with a fork and refreeze it again before serving.

To achieve the perfect granita, there is no substitute for the fork technique.

Serves 4

yorkshire puddings.

Traditionally served with roast beef, Yorkshire pudding
is a speciality from the north of England.

2 cups plain (all-purpose) flour

1/2 teaspoon salt

3 eggs, lightly beaten

2 cups milk

oil, dripping or lard

Sift the flour and salt into a mixing bowl. Make a well in the centre and add the beaten
eggs. Mix with a wooden spoon and gradually add the milk, beating until smooth.

Leave the batter to rest for at least 1 hour.

Preheat the oven to 220°C (425°F, Gas Mark 7).

Use individual Yorkshire pudding tins or muffin tins. Put 1/2 teaspoon of oil, dripping
or lard into each individual tin. Place in the oven for 5 minutes, or until the fat is very hot
and smoking.

Pour the batter evenly into the tins, return to the oven and cook on the top shelf for
15–20 minutes, or until risen and golden. Don't be tempted to open the oven before
they're ready, otherwise they will collapse.

*Resting the batter is crucial. It allows the starch in the flour to swell, which bursts
when it hits the hot oil, giving a light texture.*

*For perfect timing when cooking a roast, allow the meat to cook and then remove from
the oven. Increase the heat and cook the puddings while the meat is resting.*

*You can make one large Yorkshire pudding in a roasting tin, if you like. In this case,
spoon 2 tablespoons of oil, dripping or lard into the tin to heat. Pour in the batter and cook
for 35–40 minutes, or until risen and golden.*

Makes 12

conversions.

All cup and spoon measurements are level.

I use 60 g (2 oz, grade 3) eggs.

All recipes were tested using a regular convection oven. If you are using a fan-forced oven, set your oven temperature to approximately 20°C (70°F) lower than is recommended in the recipe.

Cup conversions

1 cup uncooked arborio rice = 220 g (7 oz)

1 cup uncooked basmati/long-grain rice = 200 g (6$^1/_2$ oz)

1 cup sugar = 250 g (8 oz)

1 cup brown sugar = 185 g (6 oz)

1 cup caster (superfine) sugar = 250 g (8 oz)

1 cup icing (confectioners') sugar = 250 g (8 oz)

1 cup chopped pecans = 125 g (4 oz)

1 cup plain or self-raising (self-rising) flour = 150 g (5 oz)

1 cup cornflour (cornstarch) = 150 g (5 oz)

1 cup uncooked couscous = 180 g (6 oz)

1 cup grated mozzarella = 150 g (5 oz)

1 cup grated parmesan = 100 g (3$^1/_2$ oz)

Liquid conversions

metric	imperial	standard cups
30 ml	1 fl oz	2 tablespoons
60 ml	2 fl oz	$^1/_4$ cup
80 ml	2$^3/_4$ fl oz	$^1/_3$ cup
125 ml	4 fl oz	$^1/_2$ cup
185 ml	6 fl oz	$^3/_4$ cup
250 ml	8 fl oz	1 cup

Dry measurements

metric	imperial
15 g	$^1/_2$ oz
30 g	1 oz
45 g	1$^1/_2$ oz
55 g	2 oz
125 g	4 oz
150 g	5 oz
200 g	6$^1/_2$ oz
225 g	7 oz
250 g	8 oz
500 g	1 lb
1 kg	2 lb

Oven temperatures

Celsius		Fahrenheit	Gas Mark
120°C	very slow	250°F	1
150°C	slow	300°F	2
160°C	warm	315°F	2–3
180°C	moderate	350°F	4
190°C	moderately hot	375°F	5
200°C	moderately hot	400°F	6
220°C	hot	425°F	7
230°C	very hot	450°F	8
240°C	very hot	475°F	9

index.

acknowledgements.

Firstly I want to express my thanks to Cathy Osmond, the inspired editor of the 'Review' section of the Weekend Australian, *and to Rosie Higson, who has taken Cathy's place while Cathy is on maternity leave.*

Big hugs and much gratitude to the friendly team at Penguin Australia, especially Julie Gibbs, a brave and optimistic soul for taking me on, and to Jane Morrow, my wonderful editor, who has made sense of my mutterings, scribblings and frantic emails. To Louise Leffler for her great design and for holding my hand at the shoot.

I also want to send three big cheers to Andre Martin for his patience, talent and great pictures. To Mary Harris for her treasure trove of props and good things in cupboards. To Susie for once again letting me take over her house, and to Francis for his humour, friendship, wisdom and love of eating.